# HBCU
## Healthcare
## Pathways

RISING SUN PUBLISHING

# HBCU

## Healthcare Pathways

## MYCHAL WYNN

### VOL II: WHY ATTEND AN HBCU SERIES

# HBCU Healthcare Pathways
## *Vol II: Why Attend an HBCU series*



Mychal-David Wynn, Editor
David Escobar, Cover Design

RISING SUN
PUBLISHING

P.O. Box 70906
Marietta, GA 30007
(770) 518-3069
E-mail: info@rspublishing.com
Website: www.rspublishing.com

Printed in the United States of America.

# Acknowledgments

I would like to acknowledge my wife, Nina, who has committed herself and joined me in my efforts over the course of many years, to expand the college and scholarship outcomes of students from throughout the United States. Between the many prayers, prayed on behalf of students and families, and the thousands of text messages exchanged with students and parents, she has availed herself 24/7 to help others.

I would like to acknowledge my good friend, and retired California Community College professor, Dr. Karen McCord, who is a relentless advocate for students. It was her phone call inviting me to support the California Community Colleges Guaranteed HBCU Transfer Pathways that was the catalyst for the *Why Attend an HBCU* series of books.

I would also like to thank my son and editor, Mychal-David Wynn, who has a BA in English from Amherst College and who has committed his literary expertise to not only supporting our work, but editing essays of hundreds of students to ensure they present their best writing in their college and scholarship applications.

## Dedication

This book is dedicated to those who are advocating for equity and opportunity—the founding principal of Historically Black Colleges and Universities.

"Give someone a fish, and you feed them for a day. Teach someone to fish, and you feed them for a lifetime."

# Table of Contents


Foreword ...................................................................vii

A Student's Perspective—Erin N. .............................xiii

Introduction ......................................................... xvii

Who Will Benefit Most From This Book? ......................1

Which HBCU is Right for You? ....................................8

Healthcare Pathways can be Expensive ................... 13

HBCU Chiropractic Pathways.................................... 23

HBCU Dental Pathways............................................. 29

HBCU Medical School Pathways................................ 40

HBCU Nursing Pathways ........................................... 56

HBCU Optometry Pathways ..................................... 71

HBCU Pharmacy Pathways ....................................... 83

HBCU Physical Therapy Pathways ............................ 92

HBCU Podiatry Pathways ........................................ 103

HBCU Veterinary Pathways......................................106

In Summary............................................................. 111

Appendix: HBCU Listing ..........................................117

References .............................................................. 121

Tables .................................................................... 129

Index...................................................................... 131

# Foreword

Data from the U.S. Bureau of Labor Statistics Occupational Outlook Handbook, *"Healthcare Occupations,"* projects that overall employment in healthcare occupations will grow much faster than the average for all occupations from 2022 to 2032. About 1.8 million openings are projected each year, on average, in these occupations. The median annual wage for healthcare practitioners and technical occupations (such as physicians and surgeons, registered nurses, dental hygienists, and clinical technicians) was $80,820 in May 2023, which was higher than the median annual wage for all occupations of $48,060.

| | |
|---|---|
| Chiropractors: $76,530 | Optometric Technicians: $56,450 |
| Clinical Technicians: $60,780 | Opticians: $44,170 |
| Dentists: $170,910 | Pharmacists: $136,030 |
| Dental Hygienists: $87,530 | Pharmacy Technicians: $40,300 |
| Dietitians/Nutritionists: $69,680 | Physical Therapists: $99,710 |
| Licensed Practical Nurses: $59,730 | Physical Therapist Aides: $58,740 |
| Medical Sonographers: $80,850 | Physicians & Surgeons: $239,200[+] |
| Nurse Anesthetists: $129,480 | Podiatrists: $141,650 |
| Occupational Therapists: $96,370 | Registered Nurses: $86,070 |
| OT Assistants: $65,450 | Veterinarians: $119,100 |
| Optometrists: $131,860 | Veterinary Technicians: $43,740 |

HBCUs have had, and continue to have, an important role in diversifying the workforce and ensuring that Blacks have equitable access to these jobs. The National Center for Health Workforce Analysis *"State of the U.S. Health Care Workforce, 2023,"* reports that while Blacks make up 12 percent of the U.S. population, they are disproportionately underrepresented in virtually all healthcare fields, as reflected in the table on the following page.

| Occupation | Percentage of Blacks |
| --- | --- |
| Audiologists | 3.4% |
| Cardiovascular Technicians | 8.2% |
| Chiropractors | 2.7% |
| Clinical Lab Technicians | 16.1% |
| Dentists | 4.1% |
| Dental Hygienists | 3.9% |
| Dental Assistants | 6.8% |
| Dietitians and Nutritionists | 12.1% |
| EMTs and Paramedics | 6.9% |
| Nurses | 13.7% |
| Optometrists | 1.9% |
| Pharmacists | 6.5% |
| Physician Assistants | 5.3% |
| Podiatrists | <1% |
| Psychologists | 6% |
| Occupational Therapists | 5.2% |
| Opticians | 6.3% |
| Pharmacy Technicians | 13.6% |
| Physical Therapists | 4.1% |
| Radiation Therapists | 6.6% |
| Recreational Therapists | 13.3% |
| Respiratory Therapists | 13.2% |
| Speech-language Pathologists | 4.9% |
| Veterinarians | 1.5% |

Since pursuing a healthcare career pathway will not be easy, consider pursuing an area of study for which you are passionate and within which there are alternative career pathways. For example, during a recent eye exam, I talked to the Optometric Technician who loved her job and I talked to the Optometrist, who loved her job. Both the technician and the optometrist were not only working in a field that they loved, but one which offered further pathways to additional certifications and degrees.

Pursuing a healthcare pathway will require long hours of studying math and science, which unfortunately, many students will leave high school inadequately prepared to succeed in entry-level college math and science coursework. Even straight 'A' students who have taken the highest-level math and science classes available at their high school, may find themselves ill-prepared for the rigor and pace of college-level math and science. Despite students' entering college ill-prepared, HBCUs have a history of success with students pursuing careers in healthcare and America needs more diversity in healthcare.

The Haverford College article, *"Why the U.S. Needs More Black Physicians,"* shares an encounter between Dr. James Carter, a Black doctor, and a patient:

> The woman sat up and stared as James Carter entered her hospital room. Her mouth opened, but no words came out. Finally, he asked what she was looking at. "I had no idea there were Black doctors on this campus," she replied. Carter, a cardiologist specializing in wound care at University of Colorado Hospital, has been practicing medicine for more than three decades—but this encounter didn't take place early in his career. It happened last year.
>
> As the United States faces a racial reckoning, glaring inequities among medical professionals persist, with Black physicians remaining particularly scarce. In 2003, when a landmark Institute of Medicine report called for an increase in minority healthcare workers to address long standing health disparities, Black people represented 12.4 percent of U.S. residents and 3.3 percent of physicians. Nearly 20 years later, Black Americans still make up 12.4 percent of the population— and only 5 percent of physicians. Haverford alumni working in medicine can attest that although the factors perpetuating the physician workforce gap are complex, they intersect to produce one clear-cut consequence: poorer health outcomes for Black individuals.

Williams and Mullan in their STAT News article, *"Why we need more Black doctors,"* write:

> Cultural competence plays an important role in communication that goes far beyond diagnostic skill. It encompasses the knowledge, skills, and attitudes required to bridge cultural, ethnic, and linguistic gaps between patients and providers. It's not a once-and-done module or in-service training but a lifelong pursuit.

There are consequences to cultural incompetence. In one study, Black patients nearing the end of their lives received much less empathy from white physicians than from their Black counterparts, despite receiving the same factual information. In an even more disturbing study, half of the medical students at the University of Virginia falsely believed that Black patients' blood coagulates faster than that of white patients and that Black people have more tolerance to pain than whites.

The study *"The association among specialty, race, ethnicity, and practice location among California physicians in diverse specialties,"* notes that underrepresented physicians of color are more likely to serve in underrepresented communities of color, (Odom Walker, Moreno, Grumbach, 2012) and there is a glaring doctor shortage in hundreds of communities that are predominately Black. Data from *"Differences in incomes of physicians in the United States by race and sex: observational study,"* also shows that Black male physicians, particularly when practicing medicine in predominately Black communities, are more likely to work in primary care, (Ly, Seabury, Jena, 2016) where there is the greatest need.

In nearly every healthcare profession presented in this book, Blacks are hugely underrepresented. Many Black students will have faced an unavoidable uphill climb as a result of their underrepresentation in high school AP and dual enrollment classes, under enrollment in high school calculus, inadequate SAT/ACT prep, and a lack of money. In virtually every possible way, the odds have been stacked against Black student success in pursuing healthcare career pathways—so much so that many students will give up on their dreams prior to entering college or switch majors after entering college. Don't you dare. Don't give up on your dreams. America needs more Black healthcare professionals. America needs you to follow your dreams.

In 1992, when my wife and I moved from Carson, California to Roswell, Georgia, the first thing we did after settling into our apartment was to find a Black pediatrician for our son who was 4-years old at the time. We knew exactly where to go—Morehouse Medical School. Dr. Kevin Mason, a Morehouse College graduate, was our older son's pediatrician. 6 years later, when our younger son was born, Dr. Kevin Mason had moved into private practice and our sons' new



Mychal Wynn

pediatrician was Dr. Truddie Darden, who, in her Morehouse School of Medicine retirement statement, writes:

> *"Continue being purposeful and compassionate with patients. Be communicative. Develop the approach that helps patients to feel comfortable with you as their physician, their provider. To be comfortable sharing those things that may not be shared, that may not be disclosed, but are important to the healthcare of the patient," she advises. "That comes from building relationships and developing a level of comfort and being trusting and trustworthy as well as just being comforting."*

Today, not only are there HBCU colleges and medical schools to support students of color pursuing healthcare career pathways, there are organizations like BlackDoctors.org and Black Doctors USA providing bridges to connect Black doctors and communities.

The Howard University College of Medicine is the oldest HBCU medical school, founded in 1868 (Lloyd, 2006). Yet, after over 150 years of producing Black healthcare professionals, this may be perhaps the best time in the history of U.S. higher education for Black students to pursue healthcare careers. HBCU undergraduate programs, as well as HBCU medical schools, provide role models and support. Beyond the 4 current HBCU medical schools, many historically Black colleges and universities have early acceptance/assurance agreements with both HBCU and non-HBCU medical schools. Not only are HBCU undergraduate and medical schools among the least expensive schools to attend, there are millions of dollars in HBCU-specific STEM scholarships to support your undergraduate, graduate, and medical school education. So hold fast to your dreams and embrace the type of plans and strategies presented in this book, and through each book in the *Why Attend an HBCU* series.

# A Student's Perspective—Erin N.

*Erin, an academically accomplished high school senior (GPA 4.5; ACT 33) attending the Kennesaw Mountain High School Academy of Mathematics, Science, and Technology Magnet Program has earned leadership and community service hours as a high school intern with our foundation. Erin's most recent responsibility was serving as a researcher on this project. Erin, who has aspirations of attending medical school, shares her perspective regarding what she learned through her research.*

Prior to researching graduate school and medical school pathways through HBCUs, I had little preexisting knowledge of such HBCU pathways, specifically into medical school. When Mr. Wynn asked me to research these pathways. I believed that even if such pathways existed, they would be either out of reach for the majority of students, or scarce to find. Through my research, I have found myself to be wrong on both accounts. I was astonished to learn how successful HBCUs are in creating such pathways and how accessible they are to students who want to plan pathways into graduate school, medical school, dental school, optometry school, veterinary school, or nursing school. I am confident that such pathways also exist for law school, but that was outside of my research focus. The purpose of these pathways and partnerships is to rid students of socioeconomic barriers that prevent them from pursuing higher education and to provide assurance that if they commit themselves to doing the work to meet the admissions criteria for their desired program that they will be assured of the opportunity to fulfill their dreams.

HBCUs have partnerships with graduate schools within and outside of the United States. Several even have partnerships with Ivy League schools. These partnerships can come in the form of early assurance or dual degree programs. Early assurance for a premed student would mean that a student would get to apply to medical school early so that a medical school would be able to offer them an early decision and a guaranteed spot. For some programs, you can choose whether or not to take the MCAT. This is a great opportunity because applying to medical school is very expensive and filled with stress and uncertainty with such low medical school admissions rates. Applicants can spend thousands of dollars in transportation expenses traveling to medical schools for in-person interviews, MCAT study tools and preparation fees, exam fees, and so much more without any guarantee of being accepted into medical school. I learned that many early assurance programs invite students to all-expenses paid summer programs where they can receive a stipend, attend MCAT preparation classes, and gain research experience.

Dual degree programs allow students a guaranteed pathway to receiving an undergraduate and graduate degree, or undergraduate and medical degree. Many such programs are not only guaranteed, but take less time and cost less money than would otherwise be required. For me personally, being assured of the institution where I will earn my undergraduate degree and the institution where I will earn my graduate degree or attend medical school prior to graduating from high school allows me to plan both my long term career goals and short term academic, leadership, and community service goals.

Many HBCUs are not only amazing in the sheer number of partnerships they have developed, but the reverence with which they are referred to is nonpareil and featured on the websites of their partner institutions. Take for instance, Jumoke Dumont's article, *"50 Years of Medicine: The Brown-Tougaloo Partnership,"* which describes the Brown University-Tougaloo College partnership.

> *"For 154 years, Tougaloo College, a historically black college (HBC) in Jackson, Mississippi, has played a leading role in the education of Black scientists and health professionals in the South and beyond.*
>
> *The private liberal arts college is among the top US schools for the number of graduates with doctoral degrees in STEM fields, and its alums form 40 percent of Mississippi's African American physicians and dentists.*
>
> *Brown became an active partner in this tradition in 1976 when it established the Early Identification Program in Medicine for Tougaloo*



Mychal Wynn

*(EIP). An expansion of the historic Brown University-Tougaloo Partnership (BTP), the EIP identifies Tougaloo undergrads for early acceptance to Brown's MD program.*

*The EIP in Medicine for Tougaloo is one of the BTP's longest-standing active programs. It has produced two generations of physicians -- MDs who are leaders in their fields and the communities they serve."*

During my research, I discovered that one HBCU had partnerships with 16 graduate schools (Xavier University of Louisiana), thereby providing 16 different pathways to early assurance and dual degree programs. My research for this project dispelled any preexisting notions I previously held regarding the quality of education or scope of opportunities offered at HBCUs. I left the project with a much deeper understanding of how committed HBCUs are to not only the success of their students, but in creating leaders like Vice President, and presidential candidate Kamala Harris, who has already had a global impact. These schools work hard to ensure that after their students receive their undergraduate degree, they have the best opportunities for continuing their education into graduate school, medical school, law school, or beyond.

I hope that you will learn from reading this book, what I have learned— why HBCUs have such a rich and long history of producing Black professionals in virtually every career field from education to medicine and from the arts to STEM. The amount of support and tools HBCUs provide to help students pursue their educational and career aspirations is such an important feature of HBCUs. Based on indisputable outcome data, their strategies are arguably more effective for African American success than those of other highly selective schools.

Erin N.
Kennesaw Mountain High School Class of 2025
Academy of Mathematics, Science, and Technology

# Introduction

The fundamental principle in which this, and the other books in the *Why Attend an HBCU* series are written, is the adage,

*Give someone a fish, and you feed them for a day.*
*Teach someone to fish, and you feed them for a lifetime.*

To teach someone to fish, the teacher must be knowledgeable about the "process" of fishing. To keep from starving, the student must be willing to both learn and apply the process. Teaching a process to someone follows the principle of "backwards mapping," which means to begin with the end in mind, i.e., not starving. With not starving as the end goal, the process evolves from working backwards to plan how you will catch fish. In regard to attending an HBCU, or any college, if the goals are to pursue a career pathway, while avoiding student loan debt, then working backwards requires developing a set of strategies for identifying the right educational pathway, while making yourself a competitive candidate for being awarded enough scholarship money to avoid student loan debt.

Data from a variety of sources, reflect that students pursuing the type of healthcare pathways presented in this book on average, assume tens of thousands of dollars in student loan debt:

- $293,900 is the average student loan debt for dentists (Porter, 2023)

- $200,000 is the average medical school debt (Rivera, 2024)

- $167,711 is the average student loan debt for pharmacists (Luthi, 2024)

- $157,146 is the average student loan debt for veterinarians (Mattson, 2020)

- $152,882 is the average student loan debt for physical therapists (APTA, 2020)

Ryan Lane, in the Nerdwallet article, *"Average Nursing Student Debt: How Much Debt Do Nurses Have?"* notes the average student loan debt for Nursing is:

- $23,302 for an Associate Degree in Nursing (ADN)
- $28,917 for a Bachelor of Science in Nursing (BSN)
- $49,047 for a Master of Science in Nursing (MSN)

Based on U.S. Department of Education data, the *"Average Graduate Student Loan Debt"* (Hanson, 2024) is:

- $37,337 for a bachelor degree
- $83,651 for a master's degree
- $125,276 for a PhD

The Association of American Medical Colleges data, *"Medical Student Education: Debt, Costs, and Loan Repayment Fact Card for the Class of 2023,"* calculates that students holding $200,000 in federal student loans will accrue $159,000 in interest resulting in a total repayment amount of $359,000, taking the average practicing doctor over 17 years after completing their medical residency to repay. This huge amount of debt is being assumed by millions of students, not only by students attending HBCUs. However, the United Negro College Fund's report, *"Fewer Resources More Debt: Loan Debt Burdens Students at Historically Black Colleges & Universities,"* notes that 80 percent of students enrolling in HBCUs are using student and Parent PLUS loans to pay for undergraduate school (Saunders, 2016). When you add the student loans taken out for medical school, pharmacy school, veterinarian school, dental school, nursing school, etc., it is easy to understand how the amount of student loans can easily exceed $200,000! However, with so many HBCU-specific scholarship opportunities, attending an HBCU can be a low-debt or debt-free pathway into a well-paying and personally rewarding healthcare career with the proper planning.

Collectively, the books in the *Why Attend an HBCU* series provide comprehensive guidance in matching to the right HBCU, the right program, and the right scholarships. Pursuing healthcare pathways through an HBCU can have an indelible impact on your life years after entering into your post-college career:

- The HBCU undergraduate experience, as covered in *Why Attend an HBCU*, provides a holistic experience in culture, history, caring, and encouraging excellence in uplifting Black students in particular, and the Black community as a whole.

- The costs of attending an HBCU and the type of education received, is an important consideration for students pursuing a pathway into a healthcare career, which will include many years of schooling and the potential to have a huge impact on global communities.

- As presented in the chapter, *HBCU ED/Dual Degree Programs*, HBCUs can assist students in navigating the huge competition in pursuing healthcare pathways through guaranteed early acceptance/assurance programs into medical school, dental school, nursing school, and graduate programs.

- The plethora of HBCU-specific scholarship opportunities, as covered in *HBCU Scholarships*, provide opportunities to avoid tens of thousands of dollars in student and Parent PLUS loan debt.

- HBCUs, through their shared philosophies of leadership and service, prepare healthcare professionals to not only earn a degree, but to make a difference in patients' lives.

Maximizing the information presented in this book requires a level of intellectual curiosity driven by seeking answers to such important questions as: Which school or program is the right fit for my educational and career aspirations? Which schools are the right fit for my financial need? Which schools are the right fit for my unique situation and circumstances? Which scholarships are the right match to my body of work?

There are many such questions to be asked and answered in identifying the schools that are the right fit for earning a 4-year degree, finding undergraduate research opportunities, entering into the workforce, or preparing to attend graduate school, nursing school, dental school, or medical school. Consequently, answers to these questions may lead to a school other than a school close to your home or one of the more recognizable HBCU brands. In a manner similar to the reputation of their marching band, individual schools will have a reputation for their success in preparing students for healthcare careers and the partnerships they have established with employers of their graduates. Scholarship opportunities will also vary among schools. Even students who are committed to attending the HBCU that their parents attended, can avoid student and Parent PLUS loan debt by following the strategies presented in the *Why Attend an HBCU* series.

While we have wonderful HBCUs in the Atlanta University Center here in Georgia, we have worked with many students who found their full institutional scholarship opportunities at such schools as Benedict College, Claflin University, Florida A&M University, Hampton University, Howard University, North Carolina A&T State University, North Carolina Central University, Tennessee State University, Tuskegee University, and Xavier University of Louisiana. Students like our son, who is a 2012 Gates Millennium Scholar, who attended Morehouse College, were able to expand their list of schools and avoid student loan debt through private scholarships.

While HBCUs share many commonalities, they are no more homogeneous than is the Black community. They represent public and private institutions. Public institutions rely primarily on funding from state legislatures and are governed by boards appointed by the governor of their state. Private institutions tend to be smaller and more personalized. Some schools guarantee on-campus housing for all four years, while other schools only guarantee on-campus housing for first-year students. Recently, *ABC 11 News Raleigh NC (WTVD)* reported that North Carolina Central University was unable to guarantee non-freshmen housing for the 2024-25 academic year:

> *NCCU has received 25.88% more applications for first-time, first-year students enrolling in Fall 2024 than for Fall 2023 at this time last year. All freshmen students who applied and made the required deposits by May 8, 2024, are guaranteed on-campus housing. As for continuing students, housing will be on a first-come, first served basis. The university has asked students to consider off-campus housing. If freshmen students choose to not attend, their housing will be re-allocated to continuing students.*

As HBCU applications increase, it is becoming increasingly difficult to gain admission to private HBCUs like Clark Atlanta University, Hampton University, Tuskegee University, Morehouse College, and Spelman College. According to the U.S. Department of Education's College Scorecard, while the acceptance rate at Alabama State University, a public university, is 97 percent, 42 miles away, the acceptance rate at Tuskegee University is only 30 percent. Similarly, while the acceptance rate at Morgan State University, a public university, is 85 percent, 678 miles away, the acceptance rate at Spelman College is only 28 percent. While this book will provide guidance in identifying HBCUs and programs, which best match to your educational and career aspirations, you must commit yourself to the work needed to gain admission into these programs.

As you identify college majors or programs of interest, the following websites should prove helpful in identifying the HBCUs offering the major in which you are interested:

- College Factual, a website where you can take a quick look at any HBCU and explore a variety of college majors and degree programs

- CollegeBoard BigFuture, a website providing similar information and AP credit policies for each school

- findmyhbcu.com, a website providing information about colleges and programs

- HBCU First, provides insight into the HBCU community and lists HBCUs by state and provide videos of many campuses

- National Center for Education Statistics College Navigator, provides information about all accredited colleges and universities in the United States

- The Hundred-Seven, a website providing information about the programs and majors offered specifically at HBCUs

- U.S. Department of Education College Scorecard, provides comprehensive information about all accredited colleges and universities in the United States and allows comparing up to ten colleges side-by-side

*James McCune Smith was the first African American to earn a medical degree (Greene, 2021), educated at the University of Glasgow in the 1830s, when no American university would admit him. Smith was also one of the nation's leading abolitionists. In 1859, Frederick Douglass declared, "No man in this country more thoroughly understands the whole struggle between freedom and slavery than does Dr. Smith, and his heart is as broad as his understanding."*

*— James McCune Smith, MD (1813 — 1865)*

# Who Will Benefit Most From This Book?

E ach of the books in the *Why Attend an HBCU* series is focused on informing students, parents, teachers, counselors, coaches, and college advisers by providing insight into the many, cultural, educational, and career pathways through HBCUs and into the workforce. The goal is not to convince a student of where he or she should attend college, but to share information about the opportunities at HBCUs that are often not fully understood, or misunderstood. Each student should pursue the career or college pathway reflective of their gifts, talents, interests, and financial need. For many students, HBCUs may offer unique options, opportunities, workplace pathways, and accessibility to scholarships.

If you are a student who is intellectually curious and who wants to know the facts so that you can plan your best pathway toward your dreams and aspirations, then this book will serve as an invaluable resource. A parent or counselor who wants to know the facts regarding the unique opportunities and unparalleled support offered students pursuing healthcare pathways through HBCUs will find a plethora of educational facts and occupational data. The Teachers College at Columbia University, in the article *"What HBCUs Can Teach Us About Culturally Sustaining Practices,"* (Brathwaite, et al., 2021) shares research validating the success of HBCUs:

> Recent CCRC research found that few U.S. colleges have implemented culturally sustaining practices in a comprehensive way. But Historically Black Colleges and Universities (HBCUs) and other minority serving institutions gave us our best sense of what a college imbued with culturally sustaining practices could look like and provided evidence for the value of the practices. HBCUs graduated 46% of Black women who earned degrees in STEM disciplines between 1995 and 2004. Of all the bachelor's degrees earned by African Americans in STEM fields, 25% were earned at HBCUs. The success of HBCUs has been attributed to their strong leadership and dedicated faculty and staff.

Despite inadequate funding and a marginalized status in higher education, HBCUs have been able to create a humanistic environment for student learning. Students feel that college faculty and staff value their presence as individuals and have a shared sense of commitment to their success. In 2020, The National Science Foundation created the HBCU STEM Undergraduate Success Research Center to better understand HBCUs' success and to implement promising practices more widely.

Anyone planning to pursue a career in healthcare must pause and consider the importance of healthcare related careers, as well as the cost of the level of education required depending on your desired healthcare career pathway. Whether your aspirations are to become a medical researcher, medical doctor, dentist, nurse, psychiatrist, physical therapist, or pharmacist, these are all fields that can have life or death implications. To some degree, each field requires precision, whether in-patient diagnosis, physical examination, prescribing medication, recommending lifestyle changes, performing surgery, or supporting rehabilitation.

## Preparation for the Workforce

To successfully go through years of academic preparation and training requires high levels of discipline, an appropriate temperament, a growth mindset, and grit. Such qualities do not reveal themselves AFTER you become a medical professional, but years prior in how you approach listening, learning, and doing—particularly in math and science. Each level of learning becomes deeper and more intense. While these transitions are experienced in the transition from elementary school to middle school and from middle school to high school, they magnify in the transition from high school to college. So much so that many students are better served by choosing a pathway through a 2-year technical school or community college to equip themselves with the study skills and learning strategies needed to make a successful transition into a 4-year college or university.

Math and science at the college level, even for the student who has taken such classes as *AP Calculus AB* and *AP Calculus BC*; or *AP Physics, AP Chemistry,* or *AP Environmental Science* in high school can be daunting. College-level professors have an expectation



Mychal Wynn

that students demonstrate the ability to apply knowledge beyond simply responding to multiple-choice questions or solving problems based on what has been taught in the classroom. The expectation is for students to take what has been taught and demonstrate learning by applying the information to new situations. In many college classes, you may have only 3 opportunities, which will determine your final grade—a paper or project, a midterm exam, and a final exam.

Unlike high school classes where students and parents are able to lobby for additional opportunities or where schools have policies that do not allow teachers to issue a failing grade unless a student has had multiple opportunities to retake an exam or turn in late assignments, college will be different and college professors less accommodating. Yet, among all colleges, HBCUs have an extensively researched and well documented history of providing the level of transitional support and remedial classes needed to help students rise to college-level academic expectations.

While the language of math is difficult to understand for many students, math is considered the most critical high school subject by many colleges and universities due to the critical-thinking and problem-solving skills taught in math and applicable to every discipline, both STEM and non-STEM. Many colleges and universities view calculus as a gateway class—one that is required for students to be considered for admission, even for non-STEM majors. Data from the National Center for Education Statistics, "*Advanced mathematics and science courses,*" reports that less than 2 in 10 (16%) high school students take calculus. The National Center for Education Statistics reports the following racial disparities in calculus course taking: (Indicator 13)

- 45% of Asian students take calculus
- 18% of White students take calculus
- 10% of Hispanic students take calculus
- 6% of Black students take calculus

Students who do not take calculus in high school often find themselves at a disadvantage in their *Introduction to Calculus* class in college where the class moves at a fast pace and professors expect students to have a foundational understanding of calculus.

The *University of California's 2024 Statement on Mathematics* notes:

> A student intending a STEM major (including Data Science or Computer Science) at the college level is well-advised to take Calculus or Pre-calculus, whereas others may find courses such as AP Statistics more useful.

For students pursuing any STEM career pathway, including healthcare, higher level math and science are stepping stones for being offered admission to college, accepted into your major, preparation for your academic curriculum in college, and then as part of the comprehensive knowledge you are expected to demonstrate on the MCAT and various licensing exams.

Veronica Anderson's report, *"A New Calculus for College Admissions: How Policy, Practice, and Perceptions of High School Math Education Limit Equitable Access to College,"* notes one admission officer as saying:

> *"Calculus is an easy answer to a complicated question. Institutions are looking for a simple gatekeeper. We are looking for ways to determine excellent and extraordinary students." (p. 8)*

The report also notes:

> At many highly selective colleges and universities, a preponderance of first-year students arrive on campus with calculus under their belts, a phenomenon that exists even at a small, private, liberal arts institution. Consider Wesleyan University, where 79 percent of the incoming fall 2021 class had completed math through calculus—a rate that far exceeds the most recently documented national trends. (p. 9)

While there is less research pertaining to the importance of having taken high school calculus during the admissions process at HBCUs, all of the students with whom I have worked who were offered full scholarships to such schools as Tuskegee University, Xavier University of Louisiana, and North Carolina A&T State University took at least one year of calculus, with some students taking as many as 3 years of calculus (e.g., *AP Calculus AB*, *AP Calculus BC*, and

                                        Mychal Wynn

*Differential Calculus*). Similarly, students with whom I have worked who were offered admission to Spelman College as STEM majors, had also taken calculus in high school.

Another important consideration is that if you plan to apply for competitive STEM scholarships, you are likely to be competing with students who not only have taken calculus in high school, but who earned an 'A' in the class.

Whether or not you choose to pursue a math pathway through high school calculus, *AP Calculus AB, AP Calculus BC*, or dual enrollment college calculus, it is important to understand the aptitude in math and science needed to pursue STEM-related careers. On the ACT exam, designed to assess what students have learned throughout high school, there are college readiness benchmarks for each of the subject-areas tested. While the top score in each subject area is 36, the 2023 benchmark for being considered "college ready" is 22 in math and 23 in science.

ACT college-readiness benchmarks:

- English - 18
- Mathematics - 22
- Reading - 22
- Science - 23
- STEM - 26

In the ACT Profile Report, *"Graduating Class of 2023,"* among racial groups, only Asian students met the college readiness benchmarks for math and science.

Average ACT Math scores, by racial group:

- Asian: 24.2
- White: 20.3
- Hispanic: 17.2
- Pacific Islander: 16.4
- American Indian: 16.0
- Black: 15.8

Average ACT Science scores, by racial group:

- Asian: 23.9

- White: 21.0

- Hispanic: 17.7

- Pacific Islander: 16.8

- American Indian: 16.5

- Black: 16.3

To fully appreciate how successful HBCUs are with Black students who have the lowest levels of calculus course taking in high school and the lowest ACT scores in math and science, all of which are important academic preparation for pursuing a STEM-related discipline in college, it is important to reflect on the history of HBCUs in preparing Black students for STEM success. Wayna Wondwossen, in her National Science Foundation report, *"The science behind HBCU success,"* notes that while only enrolling 9 percent of Black undergraduate students in the U.S., HBCUs produce:

- 29.9 percent of Blacks in agriculture

- 27.8 percent of Blacks in the physical sciences

- 25.5 percent of Blacks in mathematics

- 24.7 percent of Blacks in biological sciences

- 15.7 percent of Blacks who earn science and engineering doctorates

HBCUs produce these successes by:

- Affirming the scholarship of Black people

- Creating a culture where the philosophy is to enable students to succeed, not weed them out

- Creating an institutional belief system that "it takes a village" where everyone on campus from the cafeteria to the Office of the President shares the mission and is invested in student success

- Cultivating a love of science in students who may have



Mychal Wynn

hated science in high school

- Cultivating a "can do" attitude in achieving mastery in math and science

HBCUs are so successful in preparing students to pursue careers in STEM that the National Science Foundation created the HBCU STEM Undergraduate Success Research Center (STEM-US), lead by researchers from Morehouse College, Spelman College, and Virginia State University to study and model the successful practices at HBCUs.

*The science behind HBCU success* further notes:

> Historically Black colleges and universities have proven to be extremely effective in graduating Black students, particularly in STEM. While HBCUs enroll about 9 percent of Black undergraduates in the U.S., they graduate a significantly higher percentage in critical fields such as engineering, mathematics and biological sciences. HBCUs represent seven of the top eight institutions that graduate the highest number of Black undergraduate students who go on to earn S&E [Science and Engineering] doctorates.

The importance of attending college in a culturally and academically supportive environment cannot be overemphasized. The research study, *"Black Medical Students' Sense of Belonging and Confidence in Scholastic Abilities at Historically Black vs Predominantly White Medical Schools,"* (Tiako, Wages, Perry, 2022) notes:

> That Black students at HBCUs feel like they belong more than their PWI counterparts is intuitive. Research shows that Black STEM students at PWIs feel excluded and report struggles with creating an inclusive campus climate, whereas HBCU students perceive STEM disciplines to be diverse and view their institutions as supportive.

If you are nearing the end of high school or are a community college transfer student, even if you have not taken calculus or did not meet the ACT benchmark scores in math and science, you can be comforted in knowing that if you are committed to pursuing a healthcare pathway, attending an HBCU can provide the needed support to deepen your competency in math and science and propel you into your healthcare career.

# Which HBCU is Right for You?

Nick Hillman, in his Institute for College Access & Success Brief, *"How Many Students Go Out-of-State for College?"* notes that overall, over 8 out of 10 students attend college in their own state. However, researching HBCU programs and college majors may result in attending college outside of your home state. Currently, HBCUs are located in 20 states (which includes California), the District of Columbia, and the US Virgin Islands. Following are the percentage of out-of-state students attending each of the following HBCUs, ranked as the top 8 producers of Black students who earn PhDs: (Einaudi, Gordon, Kang, 2022)

1. Howard University (98.28% out of state)
2. Spelman College (74.48% out of state)
3. Florida A&M University (20.09% out of state)
4. North Carolina A&T State University (25.62% out of state)
5. Hampton University (77.85% out of state)
6. Jackson State University (52.01% out of state)
7. Southern University and A&M College (13.89% out of state)
8. Morehouse College (78.18% out of state) (College Factual, 2024)

You will note that at these 8 HBCUs, that produce more Black students who are awarded PhDs than Harvard University (ranked #26), Cornell University (ranked #29), and Stanford University (ranked #29), the average out-of-state students attending private HBCUs is as high as 98 percent, while out-of-state students attending public HBCUs is as low as 20 percent.

During the 2023-24 academic year, the American Association of Medical Colleges reports that two HBCUs were ranked among the top 10 institutions producing Black students who were accepted into medical school, and a third institution, Spelman College, has as many Black students accepted into medical school as Harvard University (AAMC Table A-2.1, 2023):

- #1 Howard University (116)

- #3 Xavier University of Louisiana (94)

- #20 Spelman College was tied with Harvard University (43)

It is also noteworthy that the University of Maryland - Baltimore County with the Meyerhoff Scholars Program, patterned after HBCUs, was ranked #13 on the list with 49 Black students being accepted into medical school.

- Spelman and Bennett Colleges produce over half of the nation's Black women who go on to earn PhDs in all science fields (Louis, 2024).

- The top baccalaureate institutions of doctorates in the natural sciences and engineering include HBCUs such as North Carolina A&T State University, Howard University, Florida A&M University, Spelman College, and Xavier University of Louisiana (Hrabowski, 2021).

- 6 of the top 50 Employers of HBCU students and graduates are healthcare companies: (HBCU Connect, 2024)
  - Pfizer
  - Bristol Myers Squibb
  - Hackensack Meridian Health
  - Maximus
  - UVA Health
  - Cardinal Health

The research paper, *"HBCU and the Production of Doctors,"* (Gasman, Smith, et al., 2017) provides insight into some of the contributors to the success of HBCUs in producing Black doctors:

Considered a leader in the STEM community, Xavier has two programs that have a significant impact on premedical education: its peer- and instructor-led drill system and its peer-led student tutoring centers. Both programs were developed for students enrolled in General and Organic Chemistry, courses that see high attrition among Black students. The peer- and instructor-led drill system monitors student progress as well as provides constant reinforcement of concepts and skills with two-hour drill classes once per week. Peer-led tutoring is an institutionalized practice at Xavier. Selected by faculty, peer tutors are available throughout the day at centers on campus, ensuring students have ample access to support.

From the point of view of students, if they attend Xavier, they are confident and assured in their ability to become a doctor. They have no doubts about their future. Xavier's track record is well known among prospective students and is communicated with large billboards around the campus and throughout the surrounding states. African American communities know of Xavier's record of success in medicine. Of its nearly 3,000 undergraduate student body, 20 percent are pursuing degrees in chemistry, a subject matter critical to meet admissions requirements for medical and other health professional schools. Students know that success has come before them and that they will be the demonstrated success for those in the future. Felecia, a sophomore, shared her reasons for coming to Xavier,

*"I came to Xavier because I had a cousin who came, and then she told me how good they were with science programs, and that they were really geared towards getting people into medical school. I just felt like for me it was the best option to get myself into medical school."*

Students understand the history of Xavier and how this history will propel them to individual success. Another student, Dafina, explained it to us in this way,

*"One of the main driving points for me coming to Xavier was their success rate. Every time Xavier was mentioned, every time I say I go to Xavier University in Louisiana, people say oh you want to become a doctor, because they just know that Xavier University breeds doctors, successful doctors, all over the country. We are successful in every aspect, and every region, all over the world. So I know that, to me, that is what, every time I'm studying, I say okay, it's been done before, I can do this, and I just have to keep going."*

Xavier's first-year students have an average GPA of 3.37 and an average SAT combined math & verbal score of 985. Moreover, 57 percent of the institution's first year students are Pell Grant recipients. These statistics are not the norm for premedical students at colleges and universities across the nation. In 2015, 31 percent of newly enrolled Black students in medical school came from homes with a total income of less than $50,000. This stands in stark contrast with just nine percent of White students in a similar social class (American

Association of Medical Colleges, 2017). Xavier, with fewer resources, takes the risk and succeeds in a way that fosters future success and hope in the minds of African Americans (Gasman, 2017).

Not only does Xavier cultivate an environment where students excel, they have many early acceptance/assurance partnerships with medical schools (see *HBCU EA/Dual Degree Programs*).

Hampton University, another HBCU with early acceptance/assurance agreements with medical schools, is part of the Hampton University/Virginia-Nebraska Alliance. The primary goal of the alliance is to increase the diversity of health professionals and researchers to more equitably represent the diversity of the U.S. and global populations. HBCUs in the State of Virginia have joined with predominantly white health science education centers in the States of Virginia and Nebraska to systematically address the issues of disparities in health outcomes, and the lack of greater racial diversity within the health professional community.

When considering pathways into healthcare through HBCUs, you should focus your research on the school after you have a general idea of the level of education that you need to complete for the healthcare career you are pursuing. Many important and well paying healthcare careers do not require attending medical school.

Maryalene LaPonsie in her U.S. News and World Reports article, *"The Best HealthCare Jobs That Don't Require Medical School,"* notes the following healthcare careers, which do not require attending medical school that have median average salaries between $62K - $183K:

- Diagnostic Medical Sonographer
- Nurse Anesthetist
- Nurse Practitioner
- Occupational Therapist
- Physician Assistant
- Registered Nurse
- Respiratory Therapist
- Speech-Language Pathologist

Given the wide range of potential healthcare career pathways, it is advisable to allow "What if" questions to guide your college research.

*"What if I change my mind about majoring in biology?"* If you are passionate about science, then you may want to identify colleges with a broad range of science majors.

*"What if I change my mind about pursuing a career as a pediatrician?"* If you are passionate about working with small children, then beyond being a pediatrician, you might want to identify colleges that also offer early childhood, or child psychology programs as well.

*"What if I change my mind about pursuing a career as a dentist?"* If you are passionate about dentistry, then you might want to identify colleges with dental hygienist or dental technology options.

Considering majors beyond your first choice major is not only good strategy, but supported by data from the National Center for Education Statistics study, *"Beginning College Students Who Change Their Majors Within 3 Years of Enrollment,"* regarding how frequently students change majors:

- 52 percent of students whose original declared major was mathematics switched majors within 3 years. Students majoring in mathematics changed majors at a rate higher than that of students in all other fields, both STEM and non-STEM, except the natural sciences.

- 40 percent of students whose original declared major was natural sciences switched majors within 3 years.

- 32 percent of students whose original declared major was engineering and engineering technology switched majors within 3 years.

- 28 percent of students whose original declared major was in computer and information sciences switched majors within 3 years.

For many students, college is the first time they will have the opportunity to engage in learning what is actually required for pursuing a particular career pathway, including what they will be expected to know, what they will be expected to do, and the type of environment they will be working in over the course of a good part of their adult life.

# Healthcare Pathways can be Expensive

4 years of undergraduate school at Xavier University of Louisiana, (Tuition and Fees, 2024) one of the most successful institutions in America for producing undergraduate students of color who go on to attend medical school, costs $46,875 per year, which would amount to $187,500 over 4 years. In contrast, the cost to attend Harvard University is $82,866 per year, (Tuition and Fees, 2024) which would amount to $331,464 over 4 years. Not only in a side-by-side cost comparison, would attending Xavier be $143,964 less than attending Harvard, Harvard does not offer merit-based scholarships. Consequently, a student with high grades and test scores could qualify for Xavier's Board of Trustees Scholarship (Academic Scholarships, 2024), which would make the value of Xavier's full scholarship $331,464 less than attending Harvard.

*Note: It should be noted that Harvard, like all 8 Ivy League schools, has a need-based financial aid policy, (How Aid Works, 2024) which could provide a student from a lower income family a full need-based scholarship.*

Beyond the cost difference between Xavier and Harvard, as of the writing of this book, Xavier has 16 early acceptance/assurance agreements with medical schools (including Dartmouth, Baylor, Penn, USC, Michigan State, and Tulane), while Harvard has no such agreements. At Xavier, like other HBCUs, students who are not awarded a full scholarship upon entering Xavier have access to a plethora of HBCU-specific scholarships through the United Negro College Fund (UNCF) and Thurgood Marshall College Fund (TMCF) after enrolling. While Xavier is the example presented here, there are many HBCUs with great medical school preparation and early acceptance/assurance agreements with medical schools.

## You Need Scholarships

There is a huge disconnect between students and parents in the importance of identifying, qualifying for, submitting high quality applications to, and being awarded scholarships to pay for the costs associated with attending college, graduate school, and medical school. Thousands of students each year apply to lots of colleges and hope for the best. Only after receiving financial aid award letters, which fall far short of paying for college, students have no choice but to rely on student and Parent PLUS loans, a process that continues into graduate school and medical school. The adage failing to plan is planning to fail—or in this case, *planning to assume tens of thousands of dollars in student and Parent PLUS loan debt* is a predictably unfortunate outcome.

## First: Choose the best undergraduate pathway

No matter where you attend college, during your 4 years of undergraduate school, you can pursue virtually any undergraduate major in preparation for medical school. Although many students choose to major in biology or chemistry, neither major is required for applying to medical school. While some students say that they want to be a premed major, "premed" is not a major, but a program of study that can provide a solid foundation in math and science as preparation for medical school.

Brendan Murphy in his American Medical Association article, *"Which undergrad majors are best for med school?"* notes that the most common undergraduate majors for students who attend medical school are the biological sciences, physical sciences, social sciences, humanities, specialized health sciences, and mathematics and statistics. Data compiled by the Association of American Medical Colleges, notes the percentages of 2023-24 students admitted to medical school by major:

- 52.3% of Math and Statistics majors
- 52% of Humanities majors
- 49.5% of Physical Sciences majors
- 42.6% of Social Sciences majors

- 43.4% of Biological Sciences majors
- 40.4% of Specialized Health Science majors

Dr. Tonya Fancher, an associate dean at the UC Davis School of Medicine provides insight into undergraduate majors and how medical school applicants are evaluated: (Murphy, 2021)

> *"We look for mastery in an area that a student is passionate about. That could be in the study of art or history or science, in participation in college athletics or music or dance, or in making an impact in their community."*

This means that you can choose a college, and a college major, where you will have the best financial aid opportunities. While your grades and test scores might result in a full scholarship offer from such schools as Benedict College, Claflin University, Tuskegee University, or Xavier University of Louisiana, your college major might result in a significant amount of scholarship money through one of the many UNCF (United Negro College Fund) or TMCF (Thurgood Marshall College Fund) HBCU-specific scholarship programs.

**Second: Prepare for the Opportunities**

Pursuing a healthcare career pathway through an HBCU will involve more than academic and professional training as a result of the shared focus of HBCUs to serve underrepresented communities in response to the health disparities in both access and treatment. The Howard University College of Dentistry has a mobile dental clinic that provides free dental services to underserved communities in Washington, D.C. (Childs, 2022). Meharry Medical College School of Dentistry provides wide ranging low-cost, but high quality dental services for underserved communities. Programs such as these across all areas of healthcare are not only training and producing skilled healthcare professionals, but addressing important social issues by developing empathy and understanding among students entering into the healthcare profession.

Developing an understanding of the American Association of Medical Colleges' *"Premed Competencies for Entering Medical Students"* will enable you to begin developing these competencies in high school, community college, or your undergraduate program, thereby making you a stronger applicant for being offered admission to college, graduate school, or medical school in the future. The competencies consist of 17 traits the ideal medical student should possess. The list is broken down into three groups—*pre professional competencies, thinking and reasoning competencies*, and *science competencies*. Some of those traits may be screened for in the medical school admissions process.

**Professional Competencies:**

- **Commitment to Learning and Growth:** Practices continuous personal and professional growth for improvement, including setting and communicating goals for learning and development; reflects on successes, challenges, and mistakes; pursues opportunities to improve knowledge and understanding; and asks for and incorporates feedback to learn and grow.

- **Cultural Awareness:** Appreciates how historical, sociocultural, political, and economic factors affect others' interactions, behaviors, and well-being; values diversity; and demonstrates a desire to learn about different cultures, beliefs, and values.

- **Cultural Humility:** Seeks out and engages diverse and divergent perspectives with a desire to understand and willingness to adjust one's mindset; understands a situation or idea from alternative viewpoints; reflects on one's values, beliefs, and identities and how they may affect others; reflects on and addresses bias in oneself and others; and fosters a supportive environment that values inclusivity.

- **Empathy and Compassion:** Recognizes, understands, and acknowledges others' experiences, feelings, perspectives, and reactions to situations; is sensitive to others' needs and feelings; and demonstrates a desire to help others and alleviate others' distress.

- **Ethical Responsibility to Self and Others:** Behaves with honesty and integrity; considers multiple and/or conflicting principles and values to inform decisions; adheres to ethical principles when carrying out professional obligations; resists pressure to engage in unethical behavior; and

                                        Mychal Wynn

encourages others to behave honestly and ethically.

- **Interpersonal Skills:** Demonstrates an awareness of how social and behavioral cues affect people's interactions and behaviors; adjusts behaviors appropriately in response to these cues; recognizes and manages one's emotions and understands how emotions impact others or a situation; and treats others with dignity, courtesy, and respect.

- **Oral Communication:** Effectively conveys information to others using spoken words and sentences; actively listens to understand the meaning and intent behind what others say; and recognizes potential communication barriers and adjusts approach or clarifies information as needed.

- **Reliability and Dependability:** Demonstrates accountability for performance and responsibilities to self and others; prioritizes and fulfills obligations in a timely and satisfactory manner; and understands consequences of not fulfilling one's responsibilities to self and others.

- **Resilience and Adaptability:** Perseveres in challenging, stressful, or ambiguous environments or situations by adjusting behavior or approach in response to new information, changing conditions, or unexpected obstacles, and recognizes and seeks help and support when needed; recovers from and reflects on setbacks; and balances personal well-being with responsibilities.

- **Service Orientation:** Shows a commitment to something larger than oneself; demonstrates dedication to service and a commitment to making meaningful contributions that meet the needs of communities.

- **Teamwork and Collaboration:** Collaborates with others to achieve shared goals and prioritizes shared goals; adjusts role between team member and leader based on one's own and others' expertise and experience; shares information with team members and encourages this behavior in others; and gives and accepts feedback to improve team performance.

## Science Competencies:

- **Human Behavior:** Applies knowledge of self, others, and social systems to solve problems related to the psychological, sociocultural, and biological factors that influence health and well-being.

- **Living Systems:** Applies knowledge and skill in the natural sciences to solve problems related to molecular and macro systems, including biomolecules, molecules, cells, and organs.

## Thinking and Reasoning Competencies:

- **Critical Thinking:** Uses logic and reasoning to identify the strengths and weaknesses of alternative solutions, conclusions, or approaches to problems.

- **Quantitative Reasoning:** Applies quantitative reasoning and appropriate mathematics to describe or explain phenomena in the natural world.

- **Scientific Inquiry:** Applies knowledge of the scientific process to integrate and synthesize information, solve problems, and formulate research questions and hypotheses; is facile in the language of the sciences and uses it to participate in the discourse of science and explain how scientific knowledge is discovered and validated.

- **Written Communication:** Effectively conveys information to others by using written words and sentences.

During high school you can develop and showcase these competencies through such programs as HOSA-Future Health Professionals and involvement in high school-, faith-, and community-based programs. After graduating from high school and entering college, you can develop and showcase these competencies through your involvement in programs at your community college or 4-year undergraduate school. Through the array of internship, mentorship, and research opportunities with private and government partners, you should have opportunities to build your résumé/CV in a meaningful way as to further demonstrate these competencies. These opportunities could be

                    Mychal Wynn

further expanded through such partnerships and experiences as:

- **Yale Summer Undergraduate Research Fellowship Program:** The SURF Program is intended for students with a strong desire to pursue research careers at the PhD level. Preference is given to students completing their sophomore or junior years. Applicants must exhibit outstanding academic promise and achievement.

- **University of Wisconsin Rural and Urban Scholars in Community Health:** Rural and Urban Scholars in Community Health (RUSCH), is a premed pathway program that has been developed by the University of Wisconsin School of Medicine and Public Health in partnership with four Universities of Wisconsin campuses (UW-Milwaukee, UW-Platteville, UW-Parkside and UW–Madison), Spelman College and Wisconsin's Native American college students may enroll at any campus.

- **Wisconsin Academy for Rural Medicine (WARM):** The Wisconsin Academy of Rural Medicine (WARM) focuses on admitting and training students committed to improving the health of rural communities.

- **Training in Urban Medicine and Public Health (TRIUMPH):** The University of Wisconsin School of Medicine and Public Health developed Training in Urban Medicine and Public Health (TRIUMPH), an urban training track within the MD program, in response to health inequities and chronic physician shortages in Wisconsin's urban areas.

## Third: Develop your network and plan for scholarships

Every opportunity in which you become involved is an opportunity to build a relationship, receive a recommendation letter, or make a connection to a program or scholarship opportunity. Planning for scholarships requires developing a scholarship table, which will continually evolve as you identify scholarships and application periods which may be far into the future. While high school seniors or community college students may identify scholarships for which they can apply for immediately, other scholarships may only be available to first-, second-, or third-year college students.

Consequently, these will become scholarships for which students "plan" to apply for in the future and scholarships for which students have years to make themselves competitive applicants.

**Finally: Increase your financial literacy**

Invest in your own future by knowing how to research costs (not only tuition, room, and board, but books, application fees, exam fees, personal expenses, transportation expenses, and the cost of health insurance), calculate the interest you will pay on student loans, and how much interest will accumulate over the course of college, graduate school, and medical school. Accept the responsibility of understanding which scholarships are one-time awards versus those that are renewable, as well as understanding the academic standing required to renew scholarships. While the HBCU experience will be filled with homecoming celebrations, parties, and pledging a fraternity or sorority, do not allow such experiences to distract you from your purpose for attending college or keeping the scholarships needed to pay for college.

**Graduate and Medical School Costs**

After maximizing your undergraduate experience to become a competitive candidate for being accepted into medical school, you will require a plan for paying for medical school (which further emphasizes the importance of avoiding or minimizing student loan debt during your undergraduate education). Currently, there are 4 HBCU Medical Schools, with Xavier University of Louisiana and Morgan State University planning to open medical schools in the future. All 4 of the HBCU Medical Schools have an annual cost ranging from $52,106 to $71,910 per year.

- Meharry Medical College (acceptance rate 8.1%; annual cost $59,812)

- Howard University College of Medicine (acceptance rate 5.2%; annual cost $64,838)

- Morehouse School of Medicine (acceptance rate 4.1%; annual cost $71,910)

- Charles R Drew University of Medicine and Science (acceptance rate 11.5%; annual cost $52,106)

 Mychal Wynn

HBCU undergraduates also have opportunities through early acceptance/assurance agreements into such top ranked medical schools as: (U.S. News, 2024)

- Penn (acceptance rate 3.8%)
- Mayo Clinic (acceptance rate 3.9%)
- Boston University (acceptance rate 4.2%)
- Vanderbilt (acceptance rate 4.5%)
- Baylor (acceptance rate 6%)
- Case Western Reserve (acceptance rate 6.4%)
- Washington University in St. Louis (acceptance rate 7.5%)

4 years of medical school at The Perelman School of Medicine at the University of Pennsylvania (Perelman), ranked #3 among medical schools, and one of the schools with which Xavier University of Louisiana has an early acceptance/assurance agreement, costs approximately $110,000 per year and over $440,000 over 4 years. Added to this would be the cost of 3 - 9 years of pursuing a medical specialty such as Anesthesiology, Dermatology, Emergency Medicine, or Obstetrics and Gynecology.

In addition to your lower cost option of attending an HBCU medical school, you can also consider the cost-free option of attending The Uniformed Services University F. Edward Hébert School of Medicine, which offers free tuition in exchange for a 7-year military service commitment:

The F. Edward Hébert School of Medicine was established in 1972 to assure that the Army, Navy, Air Force, and U.S. Public Health Service would have a steady supply of physician-leaders to provide the backbone for their medical corps.

Since our first graduating class of just 29 students to the now more than 8,000 USU School of Medicine alumni, our graduates are not simply doctors, researchers and scholars; they are leaders, innovators, and public servants committed to a mission far greater than themselves. They serve in vital capacities of biomedicine, and many hold key leadership positions critical to the successful operation of the military and public health systems. The roles of our graduates are diverse and far reaching, including heading terrorism and emergency response teams, serving in the White House Presidential medical detail, commanding major Military Treatment Facilities, and conducting vital research across all disciplines of medicine.

While not a totally cost-free option, the NYU Grossman School of Medicine offers an accelerated 3-year MD program and a full-tuition scholarship to every student accepted into their program. Kaiser Permanente Bernard J. Tyson School of Medicine offers free tuition through 2025 and provides grant aid to assist students with housing and living expenses.

As you consider the cost of medical school, it is prudent to take into account medical school debt. The American Association of Medical Colleges reports that the average medical school debt is $206,924, plus an average of $27,000 in premedical school debt, and an average of $15,000 in credit card debt and other loans. Planning a pathway into and through medical school should begin long prior to entering college if you are to:

- Build a résumé during high school that will make you a competitive candidate for being offered admission to the right college, right program, and awarded the right scholarships.

- Identify the right undergraduate pathway into medical, dental, chiropractic, physical therapy, optometry, pharmacy, veterinary, or nursing school.

- Build a résumé/CV during college to make you a competitive candidate for being awarded graduate school admission, scholarships, and fellowships.

 Mychal Wynn

# HBCU Chiropractic Pathways

The following table reflects information collected from the U.S. Bureau of Labor Statistics Occupational Outlook Handbook, *"Chiropractors,"* for chiropractors and related careers.

| Career | Salary | Description |
|---|---|---|
| Chiropractors | $76,530 | Chiropractors evaluate and treat patients' neuromusculoskeletal system, which includes nerves, bones, muscles, ligaments, and tendons. Chiropractors typically need a Doctor of Chiropractic (D.C.) degree. Completing a D.C. program typically takes about 4 years, in addition to at least 3 years of undergraduate study. |
| Massage Therapists | $55,310 | Massage therapists treat clients by applying pressure to manipulate the body's soft tissues and joints. Typically complete a postsecondary education that combines study and experience, although standards and requirements vary by state. Most states regulate massage therapy and require massage therapists to have a license or certification. |
| Exercise Physiologists | $54,860 | Exercise physiologists develop fitness and exercise programs to help people improve their health. Typically need a bachelor's degree in exercise science, exercise physiology, or a related field to enter the occupation. |

In 1913, Dr. Fred Rubel graduated from National School of Chiropractic as the country's first Black Doctor of Chiropractic (Brown, 2021). Now, over 100 years later, Blacks continue to be underrepresented in chiropractic medicine. The National Center for Health Workforce Analysis *State of the U.S. Health Care Workforce, 2023,"* (Table 17) reports the following racial breakdown among chiropractors.

| Race/Ethnicity | Chiropractor Workforce | U.S. Population |
|---|---|---|
| Asian, Non-Hispanic | 5.3% | 6% |
| Black, Non-Hispanic | 2.7% | 12.4% |
| Hispanic | 5.6% | 18% |
| White | 84.2% | 59% |
| Other or Multi-racial | 2.1% | 4% |

## What is a Chiropractor?

A Chiropractor is referred to as a Doctor of Chiropractic (D.C.) or Chiropractic Physician. As described by NaturalHealers, Chiropractors diagnose and treat health problems, and promote overall well being by supporting the musculoskeletal and nervous systems. Many chiropractic schools require an undergraduate degree in physical or life sciences such as biology, chemistry, or physics. Kinesiology and exercise science are also majors that provide good preparation for chiropractic school.

Johns Hopkins University describes chiropractic medicine as *"medicine that is based on the link between the alignment of the spine and the function of the body."* A core tenant of chiropractic medicine is the belief that the body has the ability to heal itself if given proper support. The word chiropractic comes from the Greek words cheir and praxis meaning hand and practice. The words refer to treatment done by the hands or hands-on therapy.

With use of manual manipulation of the spine, chiropractors believe they can improve a person's health without surgery or medicine. Some chiropractors also prescribe exercises to do at home. Chiropractors may do lab testing, diagnostic imaging, and other testing. Some also practice nutrition and complementary medicine.

                     Mychal Wynn

Treatment may involve lying on your stomach on a special table, while the chiropractor uses his or her hands and elbows to realign the spine. Chiropractic treatments have proven to be effective in treating certain lower back pain symptoms and muscle and other bone pains. Chiropractic training is not equal to the training licensed medical doctors receive, but it is extensive. Doctors of Chiropractic Medicine have had at least 3 years of college with an emphasis on biology or basic sciences. This is followed by a minimum of 4 years of training at an accredited chiropractic college.

According to the National Board of Chiropractic Examiners, training to become a chiropractor generally takes about seven to eight years of college:

- Three-Four years of undergraduate study
- Three to five years of study at a chiropractic college
- A clinical internship

According to the Association of Chiropractic Colleges, typical prerequisites for applying to chiropractic school are:

- At least 90 semester hours of undergraduate study
- At least 24 semester hours in physical and life sciences, half of which must include substantial laboratory work
- Undergraduate GPA of 3.0 or higher
- Well-rounded educational and life experience backgrounds

Dr. Poirier of the Northeast College of Health Sciences, identifies two common undergraduate academic backgrounds of students applying to chiropractic school:

> *"There are two different categories that we see the students come from. The first is more of a hard sciences or physical sciences background. The second are those who have an applied sciences background, such as exercise science or kinesiology."*

Dr. Poirier noted that each group brings with it particular strengths, relative to the study and practice of chiropractic medicine:

> *"Those in the first group may have degrees in biology or premed and tend to have a stronger foundation in the more traditional sciences.*

*They may have done more coursework in physical sciences — for example, chemistry — and do well with these topics because they have more undergrad training. We also have students who come in from the applied side of undergrad education, such as kinesiology or exercise science. These students don't typically have as much background in the fundamental sciences, but they have more training when it comes to being able to interact with others, with potential patients."*

In the United States, the Council on Chiropractic Education (CCE) provides accreditation of chiropractic programs and institutions. The curriculum for chiropractic students includes such areas of study as:

**First year:** General anatomy; Histology; Chiropractic principles; Palpation; Human physiology; Chiropractic procedures; Embryology; Neuroanatomy and neurophysiology; and Spinal anatomy.

**Second year:** Pharmacotoxicology; Pathology; Chiropractic procedures; Clinical orthopedics and neurology; Emergency care; Clinical microbiology; and Physiological therapeutics.

**Third year:** Integrated chiropractic clinical application; Radiologic positioning and technique; Clinical psychology; Pediatrics; Physiological therapeutics; Diagnostic imaging interpretation; and Obstetrics and gynecology.

**Fourth year:** In the fourth year of chiropractic college, students work a clinical internship in a chiropractor's office. In addition to treating patients under the supervision of an experienced chiropractor, many students also complete a clinical rotation at a hospital or veterans clinic.

## HBCU Pathways into Chiropractic School

The American Black Chiropractic Association (ABCA) was founded in 1981 to provide networking, mentoring, and support for Black chiropractic students and professionals. The organization sponsors scholarships, career fairs, conferences, and training.

The Council on Chiropractic Education currently recognizes 18 accredited Doctor of Chiropractic programs. Only two of these programs: Logan University and Texas Chiropractic College, have agreements with HBCUs.

**Dillard University — Texas Chiropractic College:** A 3+3 articulation agreement. Student participants will complete three years of coursework at Dillard, followed immediately by three years at TCC. Those who complete the combined curriculum will hold a bachelor of science degree from Dillard and a doctor of chiropractic degree from TCC (HBCUBuzz, 2011).

**Grambling State University — Logan University College of Chiropractic:** The "3+3 Agreement" will allow undergraduate biology majors from Grambling State University to easily transfer to the doctor of chiropractic program at Logan University. The participating students will spend three years at Grambling State University followed by another three years at Logan, after which they will graduate with both a bachelor's degree in biology and a doctor of chiropractic degree (JBHE, 2019).

You should research HBCUs with undergraduate programs in physical or life sciences such as biology, chemistry, or physics. The Howard University College of Arts and Sciences' Human Performance program prepares students across such areas as physical therapy, chiropractic, occupational therapy and exercise physiology and awards a Bachelor of Science in Human Performance.

There are many HBCUs offering degree programs in chemistry, biology, physical science, physics, kinesiology or exercise science, all of which would be good preparation for applying to chiropractic school.

A student pursuing a D.C., might also work as a Chiropractic Assistant to gain hands-on experiences working in a chiropractic setting. The type of job experiences or skills required may be:

- Knowledge of medical terminology, anatomy, and physiology
- Excellent customer service skills with the ability to provide compassionate care to patients
- Self starter attitude with strong organizational skills with attention to detail

## Resources

Governing boards, associations, and networking organizations for chiropractic medicine:

- American Academy of Orthotists and Prosthetists
- American Black Chiropractic Association
- American Board for Certification in Orthotics, Prosthetics, and Pedorthics
- American Board of Chiropractic Internists
- American Board of Chiropractic Specialties
- American Chiropractic Association
- American Chiropractic Board of Radiology
- American Chiropractic Board of Sports Physicians
- American Chiropractic Neurology Board
- American Chiropractic Rehabilitation Board
- American Orthotic and Prosthetic Association
- Association of Chiropractic Colleges
- Congress of Chiropractic State Associations
- Council of Chiropractic Acupuncture
- Council on Chiropractic Education
- International African American Prosthetics & Orthotics Coalition
- Listing of Accredited Chiropractic Schools in North America
- National Association for the Advancement of Orthotics & Prosthetics
- National Board of Chiropractic Examiners
- National Commission on Orthotic and Prosthetic Education

# HBCU Dental Pathways

Reflected in the tables is information collected from the U.S. Bureau of Labor Statistics Occupational Outlook Handbook, *"Dentists,"* regarding dentists and related careers.

| Career | Salary | Description |
| --- | --- | --- |
| Dental Specialties | $170,910 - 239,200 | There are 12 ADA-Recognized Dental Specialties: See Below |
| Dental Public Health; Endodontics; Oral and Maxillofacial Pathology; Oral and Maxillofacial Radiology; Oral and Maxillofacial Surgery; Orthodontics and Dentofacial Orthopedics; Pediatric Dentistry; Periodontics; Prosthodontics; Dental Anesthesiology; Oral Medicine; Orofacial Pain. | | |
| Dentists | $170,910 | Dentists diagnose and treat problems with patients' teeth, gums, and related parts of the mouth. Licensure requirements vary by state, although candidates usually must graduate from an accredited dental program and pass written and clinical exams. |
| Dental Hygienists | $87,530 | Dental hygienists examine patients for signs of oral diseases, such as gingivitis, and provide preventive care, including oral hygiene. Typically need an associate's degree in dental hygiene. Programs usually take 3 years to complete. All states require dental hygienists to be licensed; requirements vary by state. |

| Career | Salary | Description |
|---|---|---|
| Dental Assistants | $46,540 | Dental assistants provide patient care, take x rays, keep records, and schedule appointments. There are several possible paths to becoming a dental assistant. Some states require assistants to graduate from an accredited program and pass an exam. In other states, there are no formal educational requirements, and dental assistants learn through on-the-job training. |
| Dental and Ophthalmic Technicians | $44,640 | Dental and ophthalmic laboratory technicians and medical appliance technicians make or repair dentures, eyeglasses, prosthetics, and related products. Typically need at least a high school diploma or equivalent. They typically receive on-the-job training to attain competency. |

The consistent theme of disproportionate underrepresentation continues in dentistry where there is a huge disparity of Blacks in dentistry. The American Dental Association reports in *"The Dentist Workforce - Key Facts,"* that while Blacks comprised 12 percent of the U.S. population, they only comprise 3.8 percent of dentists. In contrast, while whites make up 60 percent of the U.S. population, they represent 70.2 percent of dentists. The National Center for Health Workforce Analysis *"State of the U.S. Health Care Workforce, 2023,"* reports the following percentages of Black dentists, dental hygienists, and dental assistants.

| Oral Health | Black |
|---|---|
| **Overall percentage of dental workforce** | **5.3%** |
| Dentists | 4.1% |
| Dental Hygienists | 3.9% |
| Dental Assistants | 6.8% |

          Mychal Wynn

The most successful pathway into dentistry for Black students is through an HBCU where 75 percent of Black dentists attend dental school (Mertz, 2017). HBCUs have a long history of preparing students to become dentists. The Meharry College School of Dentistry was founded over 130 years ago:

> Officially founded in 1886 as a department that would "provide the Colored people of the South with an opportunity for thoroughly preparing themselves for the practice of dentistry," Meharry's dental program opened its doors to nine students, three of whom were physicians, on October 4, 1886. Initial requirements for admission were that applicants needed to be at least 19 years old and of good moral character. Additionally, they were mandated to "pass a satisfactory examination in reading, writing, arithmetic, spelling, geography, and grammar, or bring satisfactory evidence of having completed a course in some recognized Normal School, Academy, or College." The basic costs of a Meharry dental education included a $30 annual fee and $10 graduation assessment. It bears mentioning that the dental department of Central Tennessee College (Meharry's first home) was launched as the first institution in the South for training African-American dentists.

Throughout its history, the Meharry Medical College School of Dentistry has had a mission of service. The current Meharry Medical College School of Dentistry vision statement is:

> *"To identify, mentor, train, and educate a diverse group of the next generation of dental practitioners, faculty and researchers, placing special emphasis on African Americans and other people of color as well as others from disadvantaged backgrounds, who will lead our communities nationally and internationally in the advancement of oral health care."*

The Core Values of HBCUs are reflective in the type of education envisioned for students, as reflected in the Meharry College School of Dentistry Core Values:

**Integrity** – professionalism and ethics in all aspects of life

**Excellence** – producing the best at all times

**Empathy** – compassionate service for underserved and healthcare disparities

**Diversity and Inclusion** – embracing and understanding cultural differences

**Leadership** – mentoring and encouraging students to pursue leadership opportunities

In a manner akin to Meharry, Howard University shares the focus on patient care reflective of the HBCU mission across healthcare professions. Following is an excerpt from the Howard University Doctor of Dental Surgery program:

> The Howard University College of Dentistry is a teaching and patient care institution and is the fifth oldest dental school in the nation. Our dental clinics, since 1881, have provided quality patient care and service to the community. The mission of the College of Dentistry includes the education of dental practitioners and dental hygienists, research, and service to the community. Through our clinical modules, students work with faculty on a 1:5 ratio and are paired with peers in your clinical level to ensure a team based approach to learning.

> The Howard student is dedicated to making a difference in Truth and Service. We emphasize evidence-based dentistry, take great pride in providing care for the underserved, and promote the highest form ethical decision making and execution of dental care. The appreciation and cultivation of service are essential to Howard dental education. Our Alumni are exemplars, mentors, and leaders in dental education, in research, in their practices, and in their communities.

While 58 percent of Black dentists who attend an HBCU dental school, attend the Howard University College of Dentistry and 42 percent attend the Meharry Medical College School of Dentistry, these are not easy schools to get into. According to International Medical Aid's report, "*Dental School Acceptance Rates: The Definitive Guide (2024)*," the acceptance rate for the Howard University College of Dentistry is only 6.51% and the acceptance rate for the Meharry Medical College School of Dentistry is even less at 2.9%. To compete for acceptance into these, and other top dental schools, students must enter college with a plan to develop a stellar academic record, demonstrate leadership, pursue internships, and make a commitment to engaging in meaningful community service—all with the goal of developing a competitive dental school application. The American Dental Education Association



Mychal Wynn

advises that to become a competitive dental applicant, you must:

- Prepare for your dental school interview
- Research dental schools by state
- Develop a high quality personal statement
- Make your application stand out

**Dental Degree Levels**

**Doctor of Dental Surgery (D.D.S.) and Doctor of Dental Medicine (D.M.D.):** The American Dental Association recognizes these as the same degrees. The designation as a D.D.S. or D.M.D. is based on the dental school that you attend.

**Associate of Applied Science (AAS) in Dental Hygiene:** Tennessee State University's AAS in Dental Hygiene Program outlines the general educational requirements in social, behavioral, and biological sciences for this degree.

**Bachelor of Science in Dental Hygiene (BS):** Albany State University's Dental Hygiene Program provides a pathway through an AAS and into a BS in Dental Hygiene: Upon successful completion of the five-semester program (including one summer of study), students will be eligible to take the national written examination, and a state or regional clinical examination. Upon passing these examinations graduates will then be qualified for employment in private dental offices, hospitals, military dental clinics, local or state health departments, or may transfer the A.S. in Dental Hygiene toward a Bachelor of Science in Dental Hygiene.

**Dental Assistant:** A dental assistant may perform basic supportive dental procedures specified by the state dental practice act and by rule of the State Board of Dentistry under the direct supervision of a licensed dentist. Typical training includes phlebotomy, intravenous access, infection control, the handling of any associated medical or dental emergencies, and any other safety related topics required by the Board before performing phlebotomy and venipuncture procedures. There are many levels of certification available for students interested in becoming a dental assistant. The Dental Assisting National Board provides an overview of the various certification programs.

- **Radiography:** In order to legally operate dental X-ray equipment and perform dental radiographic procedures under the direct supervision of a licensed dentist, a dental assistant must complete a minimum number of hours of instruction, in the content areas defined by each state.

- **Expanded Duty Dental Assistant:** Holds certification allowing the performance of expanded functions under the direct supervision of a licensed dentist in most states. An Expanded Duty Dental Assistant (EDDA) must: Hold a high school diploma or its equivalent, AND hold a current Cardiopulmonary Resuscitation (CPR) certification.

**Albany State University** offers a dental hygiene program.

**North Carolina A&T State University** offers an online Dental Assistant Program.

**Southern University of Shreveport Louisiana** is an HBCU community college offering a dental hygiene program.

**Tennessee State University** offers an Associate of Applied Science in Dental Hygiene and recently received accreditation to offer a fully online Bachelor of Science Degree in Dental Hygiene through their Degree Completion program.

**HBCU Pathways into Dental School**

Guaranteed early acceptance/assurance pathways through HBCUs into dental school allow opportunities to plan your way into dental school. Following are some of the HBCU - Dental School partnerships

**Fisk University — Meharry Medical College School of Dentistry:** Fast-track dental school agreement.

**Hampton University — University of Pennsylvania:** Combined Bachelor/Dental degree program offering conditional early acceptance to qualified students from HU's Pre-Health Program, in regard to the seven-year combined degree BioDental program. Upon successful completion of their first year at UPSDM, students will receive the Bachelor of Science degree from Hampton University. To be considered for the program, applicants should have a competitive SAT or ACT score, rank in the top 10 percent of their high school class where rank is calculated, and have a GPA of 3.5 or better on a 4.0 scale.

**Lake Erie College of Osteopathic Medicine School of Dentistry:** LECOM School of Dentistry offers an early assurance program to students from Spelman College and Tuskegee University that identifies students early in their undergraduate career as potential candidates for their school of dentistry.

**Morgan State University — University of Maryland School of Dentistry:** Offers a 3+4 option dual degree program for high school graduates (or equivalent) who will attend Morgan State University for approximately three academic years and then attend the University of Maryland School of Dentistry for four academic years. After successfully completing all academic requirements at Morgan State University and the first year of Dental School, the student will be awarded a bachelor's degree from Morgan State University. Pre-dental and Premedical students should select biology or chemistry as a major. After completing all requirements for graduation at the University of Maryland, the student will be awarded the Doctor of Dental Surgery (D.D.S.).

**North Carolina A&T State University — University of North Carolina - Chapel Hill Adams School of Dentistry:** Offers a joint program.

**North Carolina Central University — Rutgers School of Dental Medicine:** Dual degree agreement for students to receive a BS degree and a DMD degree in less than the normal eight-year time frame.

**Spelman College — Lake Erie College of Osteopathic Medicine School of Dentistry:** The Spelman College Health Careers Program Health Careers Program has a partnership with the to offer an early assurance program that identifies students early in their undergraduate career as potential candidates for their school of dentistry and a partnership with The Aetna Health Professions Partnership Initiative supports a Health Disparities Clinical Summer

Research Fellowship Program to provide a clinical research and enrichment experience and an introduction to health disparities, cross-cultural issues, principles of clinical medicine and skills for public health research and interventions.

**Tuskegee University — Erie College of Osteopathic Medicine School of Dental Medicine:** Has an early acceptance/agreement.

**Xavier University of Louisiana** has Early Acceptance/Assurance Programs to the following dental schools:

- LSU Dental School

- UAB School of Dentistry

- University of Southern California Dental School

**Know the Facts and Develop a Plan**

As in pursuing any healthcare pathway, it is advisable to begin identifying scholarships as soon as you affirm a career pathway. You can begin identifying oral health scholarships on the ADHA Institute for Oral Health website. Identifying dental school scholarships is not to be taken likely. Kimber Solano in her American Dental Association report, *"HPI publishes findings into racial disparities in oral health,"* notes that in 2019 over 99% of Black dentists reported student loan debt averaging $314,360, nearly double what was reported in 2016 in the *"The Black Dentist Workforce"* at $147,99. (Mertz, et al., 2017) The *"HPI publishes findings into racial disparities in oral health"* provides insight into the challenges to be overcome and pitfalls to be avoided when pursuing a career in dentistry:

- Educational debt levels for dental school graduates vary significantly by race. More than 20 percent of Asian dentists graduate with no student debt compared to less than 1 percent of Black dentists. **Black dentists, by far, graduate with the highest levels of educational debt.**

- Among the class of 2019 dental graduates, the **average educational debt at graduation for Black dentists was $314,360.** The average for white dentists was $283,046; $286,437 for Hispanic dentists; and $225,750 for Asian dentists.

 Mychal Wynn

No matter how much you earn through a dental practice, $314,360 is a lot of student loan debt that will continue to accumulate interest. It could take your entire working life to repay such an exuberant amount of student loan debt, if you can repay it at all. Consequently, it is advisable to develop a scholarship plan well in advance of beginning dental school.

If you are willing to exchange military service for the cost of dental school, you might consider the following U.S. Navy options:

- **Navy Medicine (NM) Internship Program:** The Navy Medicine (NM) has a long history of supporting and pioneering programs dedicated to the enhancement of minority representation in science, technology, engineering and mathematics (STEM). Historically Black Colleges and Universities/Minority Serving Institutions (HBCU/MSI) provide essential collaborations for STEM career development through the rich collection of students who will become the next generation of minority professionals. The NM internship program is designed to provide interns with an interdisciplinary experience with NM Staff Corps consisting of the Medical Corps (MC), Dental Corps (DC), Medical Service Corps (MSC) and Nurse Corps (NC).

  - Must be full-time student from a participating HBCU/MSI.

  - Must be a Sophomore or Junior college student

  - Must be pursuing careers in science and/or medicine

  - Must have a minimum 3.3 grade point average

  - Upon selection, must be able to complete a favorable background investigation, in order to participate as an intern

- **Navy Dental Corps:** The Navy Dental Corps also has a program for college students or students accepted/enrolled in Dental School where practicing dentists and dental students may receive a sign-on bonus from $75,000 up to $400,000 if you qualify. Offers have many variables depending on specialty and service requirement.

- **Health Services Collegiate Program:** HSCP can provide anywhere from $157,000 to $269,000 while attending dental school. This program provides a monthly military salary at the E-6 pay grade, generous housing allowance (dependent on location), and a comprehensive benefits package while attending dental school, but does not cover the cost of tuition, in return for service as a Navy dentist after graduation. Participants incur a year-for-year of Active-Duty Obligation, serving a minimum of three years.

- **Health Professional Scholarship Program (HPSP):** HPSP scholarships are for four- or three-year periods and pay 100% full tuition and all required fees. This includes reimbursement for textbooks, small equipment items and supplies needed for study. You can also receive a monthly allowance of over $2700 for living expenses. You must be a U.S. citizen enrolled or accepted for enrollment in an ADA-accredited dental school. Participants incur a year-for-year of Active-Duty Obligation, serving a minimum commitment of three years, and begins after you complete dental school. Provides up to a $20,000 bonus (taxable) paid in three increments between first and second HPSP monthly stipend phase. Active-Duty Obligation in conjunction with HPSP is 4 years, regardless of length of HPSP participation. The HPSP AB obligation is served concurrently with the HPSP Active-Duty Obligation. You will be commissioning into the Inactive Ready Reserve (IRR) during your time in dental school.

The National Dental Association sponsors S.M.I.L.E. (Student Mentoring with Immersive Learning and Enrichment), a Healthcare Pathway Program through a partnership between Henry Schein, Inc., the National Dental Association, and other professional associations to help mentor future healthcare professionals, enhance health literacy, expand diversity in the healthcare workforce and ultimately improve health and overall outcomes in underserved communities nationwide. S.M.I.L.E. Healthcare Pathway Program takes place in July each year with a goal of expanding each year to historically diverse colleges and universities.

## Identify the Right Program/Pathway

The information presented in this section requires that you make choices. To maximize your opportunities for being offered admission to dental school, your high school record will establish you as a competitive applicant for the dual degree and early acceptance pathways into dental school. Your options include 2 HBCU dental schools and an array of dentists and dental hygienist pathways through HBCUs.

## Resources

Governing boards, associations, and networking organizations for dentists and dental hygienists:

- American Association of Dental Boards
- American Dental Association
- American Dental Education Association
- America Dental Hygienist Association
- American Student Dental Association
- Black-Owned Dental Practices
- Browngirl RDH
- Commission on Dental Accreditation
- Dental Assisting National Board
- Interstate Dental & Dental Hygiene Licensure Compact
- National Board of Dental Hygiene Examination
- National Commission on Recognition of Dental Specialties and Certifying Boards
- National Dental Association
- National Dental Hygienists Association

# HBCU Medical School Pathways

The following table reflects information collected from the U.S. Bureau of Labor Statistics Occupational Outlook Handbook, *"Physicians and Surgeons,"* regarding careers in medicine.

| Career | Salary | Description |
|---|---|---|
| Physicians and Surgeons | $239,200 | Physicians and surgeons typically need a bachelor's degree as well as a medical degree, which takes an additional 4 years to complete. Depending on their specialty, they also need 3 to 9 years in internship and residency programs. Subspecialization includes additional training in a fellowship of 1 to 3 years. |
| Physician Assistants | $130,020 | Physician assistants typically need a master's degree from an accredited program. |

As in all healthcare professions, Black doctors are underrepresented. The National Center for Health Workforce Analysis, *"State of the U.S. Health Care Workforce, 2023,"* reports the following racial breakdown among physicians.

| Race/Ethnicity | Physician Workforce | U.S. Population |
|---|---|---|
| Asian, Non-Hispanic | 21% | 6% |
| Black, Non-Hispanic | 5% | 12.4% |
| Hispanic | 7% | 18% |
| White | 63% | 59% |
| Other or Multi-racial | 3% | 4% |

Similar to the success of dental schools, the Association of American Medical Colleges reports that HBCUs have the best success in preparing Black students for applying to medical school. The table shows where each school ranks among all colleges based on the number of Black students applying to medical school and the total number of students from the school who applied to medical school in 2023-24.

| Rank | HBCU | Black Applicants | Total Applicants |
|------|------|------------------|------------------|
| #1 | Howard University | 116 | 128 |
| #3 | Xavier University (LA) | 100 | 872 |
| #19 | Spelman College | 43 | 45 |
| #24 | Florida A&M University | 38 | 39 |
| #27 | Hampton University | 36 | 36 |
| #32 | Oakwood University | 31 | 35 |
| #42 | Morehouse College | 21 | 21 |
| #44 | North Carolina A&T | 19 | 19 |
| #45 | Jackson State University | 18 | 18 |
| #46 | Prairie View A&M | 17 | 18 |
| #46 | Tuskegee University | 17 | 17 |

There are currently 4 HBCU Medical Schools with Xavier University of Louisiana and Morgan State University planning to open medical schools in the future. In 2023-24, the Association of American Medical Colleges reported that a total of 4,672 Black students applied to medical school with 1,921 being admitted for an acceptance rate of 41.1 percent. To illustrate how much more successful HBCUs are in preparing Black students for medical school, consider that Howard University prepared 116 Black students to apply to medical school, while Cornell University, the top Ivy League producer of Black students who applied to medical school, produced 47 students. Xavier University of Louisiana produced 100 Black students who applied to medical school while Johns Hopkins University produced 48 Black students. North Carolina A&T State University was tied with Rice University with both schools producing 19 Black students who applied to medical school. Prairie View A&M University and Tuskegee University were tied with Princeton University and Syracuse University with each school producing 17 Black medical school applicants.

## Medical Degree Levels

**Doctor of Medicine (M.D.) or a Doctor of Osteopathic Medicine (D.O.):** In the U.S., there are two types of degrees that lead to the practice of medicine as a physician: a Doctor of Medicine (M.D.) or a Doctor of Osteopathic Medicine (D.O.). The two degrees reflect different types of medical school training. MD-granting institutions are often called allopathic medical schools, while DOs attend osteopathic medical schools.

Brendan Murphy in his American Medical Association article, *"DO vs. MD: How much does the medical school degree type matter?"* notes that about one-quarter of U.S. medical students train at osteopathic medical schools. That number has grown significantly in recent years, with the American Association of Colleges of Osteopathic Medicine reporting that first-year enrollment at osteopathic medical schools rose by 68% between 2011–2012 and 2021–2022. That growth is, at least in part, due to the opening of additional DO-granting medical schools.

The application requirements for MD and DO programs are virtually the same, with both osteopathic and allopathic programs weighing grade-point average and Medical College Admission Test (MCAT) scores heavily. The curricular structure of both programs is largely the same, with students typically spending much of their first 12–24 months in the classroom and the majority of their training beyond that in a clinical setting.

**Physician Assistant:** PAs (physician associates/physician assistants) are licensed clinicians who practice medicine in every specialty and setting. Prospective PAs can choose from among 308 accredited master's degree level programs in the U.S. Programs take 3 academic years or 27 months, and PA candidates are also required to engage in 2,000 hours of clinical rotations as well as passing a certification exam, among other requirements.

The American Dean Association of Physician Assistants notes that at the practice level, there are likely more similarities than differences between Physician Assistants and Nurse Practitioners. However, there are two key differences:

- PAs are educated in general medicine, which offers a comprehensive view of all aspects of medicine. NPs must choose a "population focus," e.g., pediatric nurse practitioner or women's health nurse practitioner.

- PAs are trained to practice medicine using a curriculum modeled on medical school education. NPs are trained in the advanced practice of nursing.

## Physician Assistant Programs

**Morehouse School of Medicine Master of Science in Physician Assistant Studies:** The Morehouse School of Medicine (MSM) Physician Assistant (PA) program is one of the newest professional graduate programs at MSM and comes as a response to rising health care needs across Georgia and around the world. Once established, the program will bring with it workforce diversity and increased access to care in underserved rural and urban communities across Georgia.

The MSM PA Program is a 28-month, 7-semester academic professional degree program that includes basic science and clinical coursework, clinical skills training and supervised clinical practice. The program awards a Master of Science degree after completion of the 15-month didactic phase and 13-month clinical phase. All coursework must be completed within a 48-month period. Upon successful completion of this program, new graduates will be empowered to identify and address local, regional, and global health concerns.

**Hampton University — Pennsylvania State University College of Medicine Physician Assistant Program:** Eligible students in their junior year must meet with their institution's EAP advisor to be considered and apply by June 15 for early acceptance consideration.

**Howard University College of Nursing and Allied Health Sciences Department of Physician Assistant:** The mission of the Howard University Department of Physician Assistant is to educate and cultivate compassionate, competent, and culturally diverse physician assistants committed to increasing access to health care in medically underserved communities. The program will provide an exceptional educational opportunity and experience for professional and ethical students of high academic potential, with an emphasis on underrepresented minorities in medicine focusing on Black students and other minority students. The program faculty is dedicated to preparing, empowering, and training healthcare professionals who are inclusive in their delivery of care to meet the needs and have an impact on healthcare disparities in diverse populations.

**Meharry Medical College Physician Assistant Sciences:** The mission of the Meharry Medical College Physician Assistant Sciences Program is to increase the number of students from underrepresented groups in medicine (URiM) into the PA profession. Students will be equipped with the ability to demonstrate cultural humility, provide evidence-based and compassionate care to all patients they encounter, and foster a commitment to community service in underserved populations, through equity, justice and lifelong learning.

**University of Maryland Eastern Shore Physician Assistant Department:** The UMES PA Program is a 28-month, full-time graduate professional medical sciences program designed to be taken over nine consecutive semesters with a curriculum emphasis on primary care medicine and clinical methods. The program operates within The School of Pharmacy and Health Professions and trains learners to become ethical, compassionate and professional health care providers while preparing them for certification and licensing as graduate PAs. A Master of Medical Science in Physician Assistant Studies (MMS-PAS) degree is awarded upon successful program completion.

**Xavier University of Louisiana — Ochsner Health:** Xavier University of Louisiana has partnered with Ochsner Health to advance the education of its students via a new Physician Assistant (PA) Program. It is a 28-month master's degree program that has a 12-consecutive month didactic phase and will include 16 months of clinical training within the Ochsner Health.

| Medical School | Acceptance Rate |
| --- | --- |
| Baylor College of Medicine | 6.0% |
| Boston University School of Medicine | 4.2% |
| Brown University Medical School | 2.8% |
| East Carolina Brody School of Medicine | 15.5% |
| Mayo Clinic School of Medicine | 3.9% |
| Meharry Medical College School of Medicine | 1.5% |
| Morehouse School of Medicine | 1.6% |
| Tulane University Medical School | 1.2% |
| University of Connecticut Medical School | 5.0% |
| Vanderbilt School of Medicine | 5.2% |

The above table reflects the low acceptance rates of medical school applicants. Kowarski and Wood in their U.S. News & World Reports article, *"15 Medical Schools With the Highest Proportion of Black Students,"* identifies Howard University as the only ranked HBCU:

- 70% (436 Black students) - Howard University
- 19.7% (370 Black students) - University of Chicago
- 18.5% (340 Black students) - East Carolina University Brody School of Medicine
- 18.1% (492 Black students) - Wright State University
- 13.8% (893 Black students) - UNC - Chapel Hill
- 13.7% (496 Black students) - UC Davis
- 13.0% (507 Black students) - Duke University
- 12.9% (743 Black students) - UCLA
- 12.8% (592 Black students) - Emory University
- 12.6% (797 Black students) - Michigan State University
- 12.6% (871 Black students) - Temple University
- 12.0% (341 Black students) - UC Riverside
- 11.6% (577 Black students) - Columbia University
- 11.6% (814 Black students) - Ohio State University
- 11.5% (599 Black students) - Brown University

## HBCU Pathways into Medical School

The guaranteed early acceptance/assurance pathways through HBCUs into medical school allows opportunities to plan your way into medical school.

**Alpert Medical School's Early Identification Program (EIP):** Tougaloo offers premed students a route to apply for early admission. The program provides fee waivers, MCAT waivers, application support, and targeted recruiting on Tougaloo's campus. The EIP continues to be a special highlight of the partnership as one of the longest standing active programs between the institutions. The Early Identification Program (EIP) in Medicine for Tougaloo students started in 1976 as a route of admission to Brown Medical School. Outstanding students committed to a career in medicine are invited to apply for this program. Students spend a semester at Brown before entering into the Medical School.

**Boston University Chobanian & Avedisian School of Medicine Early Medical School Selection Program (EMSSP):** Prepares students to navigate the transition to medical school through rigorous undergraduate coursework, early exposure to the medical school curriculum and culture, and the development of a unique and supportive community. Admission through the EMSSP grants provisional acceptance into Boston University Chobanian & Avedisian School of Medicine at the completion of undergraduate study.

HBCU partner schools:

- Clark Atlanta University
- Dillard University
- Hampton University
- Morehouse College
- Morgan State University
- North Carolina Central University
- Spelman College
- Tougaloo College

　　　　　　　Mychal Wynn

- University of the Virgin Islands
- Virginia Union University

**Burroughs Wellcome Scholars Early Assurance Program:** The program prepares students for medical school by providing opportunities in academic enrichment, mentoring, MCAT test preparation, community-building experiences, and clinical exposure. Partner schools whose students are eligible for the Early Assurance Program are:

- Alabama A&M University
- Alabama State University
- Oakwood University
- Tuskegee University
- Stillman College

**Fisk University and Tennessee State University — Meharry School of Medicine:** Recruit, select and support the medical education of a cadre of African American students who are interested in becoming physicians or dentists.

**George Washington School of Medicine:** Available to students from Morgan State University and North Carolina A&T State University. Students must demonstrate commitment to non-science courses, have a GPA of at least 3.5 and no C's or below, and demonstrate interest in medicine. There is an interview process and if a finalist, the student must then maintain a 3.6 GPA.

**Hampton University — SUNY Upstate Medical University College of Medicine:** The Upstate Accelerated Scholars agreement allows admitted Hampton students seeking the Bachelor of Science degree to be guaranteed acceptance into Upstate's Doctor of Medicine (MD) Program if they satisfy the following eligibility requirements: An excellent high school GPA with a 90% average minimum; extracurricular activities that clearly document experience in a healthcare setting and a commitment to service work; SAT test scores of 1200 or better (combined Critical Reading & Math) or ACT test scores of 25 Composite or better.

Other Hampton University Early Acceptance and Accelerated Programs:

- American University of Antigua, College of Medicine

- Eastern Virginia Medical School

- Lincoln Memorial University DeBusk College of Osteopathic Medicine

- Macon & Joan Brock Virginia Health Sciences at Old Dominion University: Biomedical Sciences Research, MS; Biomedical Sciences, PhD; Counseling & Art Therapy; Doctor of Medicine, MD; Medical Master's MS; Pathologists' Assistant, MHS; Physician Assistant, MPA; Public Health, MPH; Surgical Assisting, MSA

- Marshall University School of Medicine

- Marshall University School of Medicine Summer Academy Program: A hands-on residential academy at the Marshall University Joan C. Edwards School of Medicine for undergraduate students who aspire to become physicians and want to prepare for medical school.

- Meharry Medical College School of Medicine

- Penn State University College of Medicine

- TCU Anne Burnett Marion School of Medicine

- Virginia Commonwealth University School of Medicine Guaranteed Admission Preferred Applicant Track.

- Virginia Tech Carilion School of Medicine/Early Identification Program: Guaranteed Admission Program providing participants who matriculate to VTCSOM with a $20,000 tuition remission scholarship for each of their four years of medical school.

**Kentucky State University — University of Kentucky Early Assurance Program:** Offered to students in the second semester of their sophomore year. Accepted students will receive assured admission to the University of Kentucky College of Medicine – Lexington campus upon successful completion of the program requirements and graduation from the university.

**Meharry Medical College School of Medicine:** Fisk University and Tennessee State partnerships recruits, selects and supports the medical education of a cadre of African American students who are interested in becoming physicians or dentists.

**North Carolina A&T — East Carolina Brody School of Medicine:** Must be a North Carolina resident, have a GPA of at least 3.5, have a SAT of at least 1270 or ACT of at least 27. If the top two students selected meet the SAT/ACT requirements th they do not have to take the MCAT. The student must want to become a physician in North Carolina.

**Oakwood University — University of Connecticut Medical School:** Students must maintain a 3.6 GPA, complete the prerequisites, have a strong MCAT score, and show demonstrated interest in the medical field through research and clinical experience.

**Penn PASS:** Allows undergraduate students to shadow physicians, participate in student-led clinics, and create support networks with faculty to prepare their transition to med school. Penn expanded the program to five HBCUs:

- Howard University
- Morehouse College
- Oakwood University
- Spelman College
- Xavier University of Louisiana

**Ross University School of Medicine:** The requirements are a GPA of at least 3.6, a letter of recommendation, completion of prerequisites, and 12 credit hours of non science classes which do not include AP credits. Students are not allowed to apply for other medical schools or else they forfeit their application.

A score of at least a 492 on the MCAT is required. Students must have a minimum GPA of 3.2 and go through an interview process.

Partnerships with the following HBCUs:

- Alabama State University
- Albany State University
- Alcorn State University
- Bethune- Cookman University
- Charles R. Drew Medical School
- Dillard University
- Florida Memorial University
- Florida A&M University
- Hampton University
- North Carolina A&T State University
- North Carolina Central University
- Oakwood University
- Prairie View A&M University
- Spelman College
- Tennessee State University
- Tuskegee University
- University of Maryland Eastern Shore

**Spelman College — Boston University School of Public Health:** The Select Scholars Program allows junior-level undergraduate students to enroll at BUSPH through accelerated placement into the Master of Public Health program.

**Spelman College — Edward Via College of Osteopathic Medicine (VCOM):** Through this partnership, Spelman students have the opportunity to gain early guaranteed acceptance through the Rocovich Scholars Program at the end of their sophomore year if they meet certain benchmarks. Students may be considered for the Interview program or for the Early Acceptance Program. This selective program is open for up to five students per year.

 Mychal Wynn

**Spelman College — Georgetown University:** The CAM Program is designed to train students to objectively assess the safety and efficacy of various complementary and alternative medicine modalities and introduce scientific rigor into understanding the mechanistic basis for CAM therapies such as acupuncture, massage, herbs and supplements, and mind-body interactions.

**Spelman College — Morehouse Medical School:** You must be recommended by Spelman's Health Council to apply. Requires an overall 3.5 GPA with a 3.4 Science GPA. Also requires a 1300+ SAT score.

**Spelman College — University of Florida College of Medicine:** The Medical Honors Program is a combined 7-year BS/MD program designed for students who are in their second year of enrollment (post-secondary education) at a 4-year accredited science degree-granting institution (the University of Florida or equivalent institution). This program is open to students who are both Florida and non-Florida residents. Students apply for admission to the MHP through the University of Florida College of Medicine Admissions Office.

**Spelman College — Vanderbilt School of Medicine:** This educational cooperation agreement supports the selection of one rising sophomore student interested in medical school and leadership. This is a highly selective program. Participation in a structured summer program that includes research and MCAT prep for three summers is required.

Other Spelman College early acceptance/agreements:

- Lake Erie College of Osteopathic Medicine Early Assurance Program
- State University of New York Upstate College of Medicine Accelerated Scholars Program (for high school seniors)
- University of Rochester Early Assurance Program
- University of Wisconsin Rural and Urban Scholars in Community Health

**Spelman College — Zucker School of Medicine:** The Zucker School of Medicine Pipeline Program is a three-year, summer intensive, academic enrichment program is designed to provide high-achieving college students who are interested in a career in medicine an opportunity for direct matriculation to the Donald and Barbara Zucker School of Medicine at Hofstra/Northwell.

**Tougaloo College — Brown University Medical School Early Identification Program (EIP):** Provides selected high-achieving students at Tougaloo College (Tougaloo College students enrolled in their sophomore year are eligible to be considered for this program) a place in the Warren Alpert School of Medicine following the student's graduation. If selected for early assurance through the EIP, students from Tougaloo College are encouraged to enroll in undergraduate courses within the Division of Biology and Medicine at Brown University and to participate in professional development activities with their future medical school classmates in the Brown University Program in Liberal Medical Education (PLME).

**Tuskegee University Early Acceptance Programs:** Tuskegee University has early acceptance/agreements with the following programs:

- Edward Via College of Osteopathic Medicine (VCOM)
- Lake Erie College of Osteopathic Medicine (LECOM)
- Ross University School of Medicine
- University of Buffalo SUNY Jacobs School of Medicine
- University of South Alabama College of Medicine

**University of Alabama at Birmingham Heersink School of Medicine:** Burroughs Wellcome Scholars Early Assurance Program: The program prepares students for medical school by providing opportunities in academic enrichment, mentoring, MCAT test preparation, community-building experiences, and clinical exposure.

Partner schools:

- Alabama A&M University
- Alabama State University

- Oakwood University
- Tuskegee University
- Stillman College

**Xavier University of Louisiana — Baylor College of Medicine:** MD/BS Program. BS/MD Program allows qualified Xavier students to participate in a collaborative Medical Track Program, including a mandatory summer program between sophomore and junior years, which facilitates assured acceptance into Baylor College of Medicine (BCM).

**Xavier University of Louisiana — Dartmouth Geisel School of Medicine:** A major within the College of Arts and Sciences, complete at least 60 semester hours at Xavier, complete specific courses, have a GPA of at least 3.5, demonstrate interest in Geisel School of Medicine by attending information sessions, and demonstrate interest in medicine by conducting research and/or clinical hours.

**Xavier University of Louisiana — Mayo Clinic School of Medicine:** Extends MD program admission to two (2) students each year from Xavier through the Xavier-Mayo Alliance, an early assurance program. Accepted students participate in an 8-week summer experience between sophomore and junior years at a Mayo Clinic destination site (Rochester, MN; Jacksonville, FL; or Phoenix/Scottsdale, AZ).

**Xavier University of Louisiana — Michigan State University SMART Initiative:** The Mission SMART (SpartanMD Acceptance Realization Track) Initiative is an enriched, interest-directed early acceptance program to the College of Human Medicine (CHM). During their junior year (or the year prior to completion of their undergraduate degree), students apply to this program as a representative of their college/university. We do not impose a limit to the number of applications received from individual partner institutions.

**Xavier University of Louisiana — SUNY Downstate Medical School:** 2-summer initiative aimed at increasing the competitiveness of prospective medical school students by providing MCAT preparation and academic support. Summer I consists of an MCAT Boot Camp, clinical shadowing, and a stipend; if summer I is conducted in-person, students must secure their own housing. Summer II is a pre-matriculation program which provides an overview of the first few weeks of medical school (stipend included). Successful EME participants who meet certain GPA and MCAT criteria are awarded conditional acceptance into SUNY Downstate College of Medicine.

**Xavier University of Louisiana — St. Louis University Medical School Pre-Medical Scholars Program:** This sophomore-year program, which offers conditional early acceptance into medical school, requires endorsement by the Premedical Office.

**Xavier University of Louisiana — Tulane University Medical School:** This sophomore-year program, which offers conditional early acceptance into medical school, requires endorsement by the Premedical Office.

### Resources

Governing boards, associations, and networking organizations for physicians:

- American Academy of Family Physicians

- American Academy of Physician Assistants

- American Board of Medical Specialties

- American Board of Pediatrics

- American College of Physicians

- American Medical Association

- American Osteopathic Association

- American Psychiatric Association

- Association of American Medical Colleges

- Association of Black Cardiologists

- Association of Black Women Physicians

- BlackDoctors.org

- BlackDoctorsUSA.com

- Black Healthcare & Medical Association

- Federation of State Medical Boards

- National Board of Physicians & Surgeons

- National Medical Association

- Society of Black Academic Surgeons

- Student National Medical Association

# HBCU Nursing Pathways

Reflected in the tables is information collected from the Nurse.org website regarding types of nursing careers. The Occupational Outlook Handbook, *"Healthcare Occupations,"* provides additional insight into the job description, work environment, educational requirement, salary, job outlook, similar occupations, and employment rates in your state for most of the careers reflected in the tables.

| Career | Salary | Description |
| --- | --- | --- |
| Certified Registered Nurse Anesthetists | $212,650 | Care for patients under anesthesia, identify patient risks, administer anesthetic and patient medication, and educate patients and families. Current - MSN, DNP, or DNAP from a CRNA program. By 2025 - DNP or DNAP from a CRNA program. |
| Physician Assistants | $130,020 | Physician assistants typically need a master's degree from an accredited program. |
| Operating Room Registered Nurses | $129,668 | Prepare OR equipment and verify its functionality, monitor patients during operations, assist surgeons, and provide pre- and post-operative patient care and education. Additional certifications include Certified Perioperative Nurse (CNOR), Certified Foundational Perioperative Nurse (CFPN), or Certified Ambulatory Surgery Nurse (CNAMB). |

| Career | Salary | Description |
| --- | --- | --- |
| Nurse Anesthetists, Nurse Midwives, and Nurse Practitioners | $129,480 | Nurse anesthetists, nurse midwives, and nurse practitioners must earn at least a master's degree in one of the APRN roles. They must also be licensed in their state and pass a national certification exam. |
| Neonatal ICU Nurses | $128,211 | Treat critically ill neonates and newborns, monitor vital signs, give medications, record newborn's recovery and progress, change diapers, and calm distressed babies. Optional certifications include CCRN® (Neonatal), RNC Certification for Neonatal Intensive Care Nursing, and Care of the Extremely Low Birth Weight Neonate Subspecialty Certification (C-ELBW). |
| Surgical Registered Nurses | $117,052 | Surgical nurse responsibilities change per role, from scrub and circulating nurses to OR directors and med-surg nurses. Additional certifications include Certified Perioperative Nurse (CNOR), Certified Foundational Perioperative Nurse (CFPN), or Certified Ambulatory Surgery Nurse (CNAMB). |
| Pediatric Nurses | $109,492 | A pediatric nurse is responsible for administering and educating about vaccines, administering medications, performing assessments, creating nursing care plans, assisting healthcare professionals with tests and procedures, monitoring vital signs, and documenting observations and findings. |

| Career | Salary | Description |
| --- | --- | --- |
| Doctoral Degree in Nursing (DNP) | $97,000 | A Doctor of Nursing Practice (DNP) is referred to as a terminal degree in nursing because there is no higher level of education available for practice-based training in nursing. Nurses who have their DNP are sought after for positions in nursing leadership focused on clinical applications and are considered key players in the future of healthcare in the United States. |
| Labor and Delivery Nurses | $96,421 | A labor and delivery nurse is responsible for timing contractions, monitoring both the baby's and mother's vital signs, administering medications, aiding in inducing labor, and identifying and assisting with handling complications. |
| Registered Nurses | $86,070 | Registered nurses (RN) usually take one of three education paths: a bachelor degree in nursing, an associate degree in nursing, or a diploma from an approved nursing program. |
| Clinical Lab Technicians | $60,780 | Clinical laboratory technologists and technicians perform medical laboratory tests for the diagnosis, treatment, and prevention of disease. Clinical laboratory technologists and technicians typically need a bachelor degree to enter the occupation. Technicians sometimes qualify for jobs with an associate degree. |

| Career | Salary | Description |
| --- | --- | --- |
| Surgical Assistants | $60,370 | Surgical assistants and technologists help with surgical operations. Surgical assistants and technologists typically need a certificate or an associate degree. |
| Licensed Practical (LPN) and Licensed Vocational Nurses (LVN) | $59,760 | Licensed practical nurses (LPNs) and licensed vocational nurses (LVNs) must complete a state-approved educational program, which typically takes about 1 year. |
| Certified Nursing Assistants (CNA) | $38,130 | Certified Nursing Assistants (CNA) provide basic care and help patients with activities of daily living. Nursing assistants often need to complete a state-approved education program and pass their state's competency exam to become licensed or certified. |

The National Center for Health Workforce Analysis *"State of the U.S. Health Care Workforce, 2023"* reports the following percentages of Black nurses among all U.S. nurses.

| Nursing | Black |
| --- | --- |
| **Overall percentage of nursing workforce** | **13.7%** |
| Registered Nurses | 11.5% |
| Licensed Practical/Vocational Nurses | 26.2% |
| Advanced Practice Registered Nurses | 7.2% |

Many high school students begin their pathway into nursing through a Certified Nursing Assistant (CNA) program. After receiving CNA certification, a CNA can provide basic patient care under the supervision of a Registered Nurse (RN) or a Licensed Practical Nurse (LPN). CNAs, who are sometimes referred to as nurse aides, patient care technicians, or nursing assistants, can complete educational education to become a Licensed Practical Nurse (LPN), which provides more responsibilities and a higher salary. CNA programs are often available to high school students at their high school or through a local technical school or community college.

**Nursing Degree Levels**

**Associate Degree in Nursing (ADN):** Depending on the state, an Associate Degree in Nursing may or may not qualify graduates for a nursing license. However, graduates of two-year programs may apply their credits toward a Bachelor of Science in Nursing. Associate's degree holders can also enter the workforce directly and gain experience as medical techs.

**Bachelor of Science in Nursing (BSN):** A nurse with a Bachelor of Science in Nursing (BSN) can apply for licensure in every state. These four-year programs teach a broad liberal arts curriculum and more advanced nursing classes compared to associate programs.

**Master of Science in Nursing (MSN):** A Master of Science in Nursing (MSN) can qualify graduates to become Nurse Practitioners, who can work independently and prescribe medication. Other types of master's degrees in nursing include education, administration, and healthcare informatics. Master's programs emphasize research methodologies and typically require 1-2 additional years of study.

**Doctor of Nursing Practice (DNP):** A Doctor of Nursing Practice (DNP) is referred to as a terminal degree in nursing because there is no higher level of education available for practice-based training in nursing. Nurses who have their DNP are sought after for positions in nursing leadership focused on clinical applications and are considered key players in the future of healthcare in the United States.

**Nursing Specialties**

**Pediatrics:** Pediatric nurses ensure that infants and children grow up to become healthy adults. Working alongside pediatricians, pediatric nurses often consult with parents about methods to raise physically and mentally healthy children.

**Geriatrics:** Geriatric nurses help older patients maintain their independence. These professionals teach patients about strength training exercises and how to manage symptoms of chronic illness.

                    Mychal Wynn

**Developmental Disabilities:** Developmental disability or special needs nurses provide care to patients with a range of developmental disabilities and challenges. These RNs assist with mobility, communication, bodily function, and the hygienic and nutritional needs of patients.

**Dermatology:** Dermatology nurses work with dermatologists to treat skin conditions, such as infections and cancer. They often take specimens and answer their patient's questions.

**Nutrition:** Nutrition nurses are experts in dietary support as it relates to specific medical conditions. They use nutritional therapies like supplements, tube feedings, or intravenous feedings to treat patients.

**School:** School nurses work in one or more schools to treat minor injuries and administer prescribed medication. These nurses also report statistics about a school's overall health, such as the percentage of students absent due to the flu.

The NursingJournal.org website provides a general overview of nursing careers, nursing programs, and resources for anyone interested in pursuing a career in nursing. Developing a foundational understanding of the variety of pathways into a nursing career whether enrolling into a program directly after graduating from high school or continuing your education from a technical or community college into a 4-year nursing program, will assist in guiding your research into HBCU nursing programs.

**Nursing Pathways**

**Tradition 4-year BSN:** A Bachelor of Science In Nursing.

**RN to BSN:** A bridge program that helps registered nurses who hold an associate's degree earn their Bachelor of Science in Nursing. (12-24 months)

**RN to MSN:** Provides a pathway to advanced practice nursing, allowing nurses with an RN license to earn a master's degree. (24-48 months)

**Direct Entry MSN:** Provides a pathway for individuals with a non-nursing bachelor's degree, a fast-track option to become Registered Nurses (RNs) and skilled nurse practitioners with leadership and research capabilities. Types of programs include Accelerated MSN, MSN Program for Non-Nurses, and MSN Program with a Specialty Track. (24-36 months)

**Accelerated BSN (ABSN):** Provides a pathway for those who hold a bachelor's degree (in almost any field) to become a Registered Nurse or earn a Bachelor of Science in Nursing. Each nursing school will have required prerequisite classes in math and science. (12-18 months)

**LPN to BSN:** Provides a pathway for a Licensed Practical Nurse (LPN) to receive a Bachelor of Science in Nursing (BSN). (24-36 months)

**Paramedic to RN:** Provides a pathway for a paramedic to become a Registered Nurse. (12-36 months)

**Do Your Research**

While websites such as nurse.org, nursejournal.org, allnurses.com, nursingprocess.org, and hbcuconnect.com have their own methods of evaluating and ranking nursing programs, you must engage in your own research. Following are some of the areas you should consider specifically pertaining to nursing:

- Review the accreditation for any nursing program at the Council for Higher Education Accreditation website

- Reputation of the school

- Faculty and program support

- Types of nursing programs offered and class sizes

- If the program is split into lower level and upper level programs, the probability of being able to continue into the upper level program

- If the program is completed in-school or through a partner school

- If the program offers specializations

- Clinical Practicum availability, requirements, and support

- Approval by the State Board of Nursing

- Program completion rate

- Pass rates on the National Council Licensure Examination (NCLEX)

- Course requirements, cost to complete program, and salary projections for degree holders

- Job placement rate

- If the state where your college will be located (and where you plan to take the NCLEX exam) is part of the Compact Nursing States with the state where you plan to begin your post-college career. You can learn more about transferring an RN License to another state at RNCareers.org.

After deciding on the type of nursing pathway that you are pursuing, you can review college rankings or perform an internet search on such phrases as "hbcu + type of nursing programs" or do a broader search on "best hbcus for nursing."

Continue your initial research on each college's website to develop your initial list of colleges and programs. The Winston-Salem State University's Bachelor of Science in Nursing web page provides an example of how nursing pathways are presented on a college's website.

**Winston-Salem State University Pre-Licensure**

**Traditional BSN:** In five semesters, complete your general education, pre-requisites and upper division nursing courses.

**Accelerated BSN:** Already have a bachelor's degree? Complete your nursing bachelor's degree in only 15 months provided that you have taken the required prerequisite coursework. Winston-Salem State's catalog lists the following prerequisite courses:

- General Biology

- Anatomy and Physiology I, II, & Lab

- General Microbiology & Lab

- General Chemistry & Lab

- Elementary Statistics
- Lifespan Development

**Paramedic to BSN:** Graduates of an accredited paramedic program can apply their clinical experience to a Bachelor of Science in Nursing at WSSU.

**LPN to BSN:** Practical nurses with a state license to practice in North Carolina and one year of direct patient care can apply their experience to a bachelor's in nursing degree.

**Winston-Salem State University Post-Licensure**

**RN to BSN:** If you are a registered nurse going back to school, you need a bachelor's degree in nursing degree program. The RN to BSN path is online and only takes three to five semesters.

**Top HBCU Nursing Programs Ranked by nurse.org:**
- Fayetteville State University School of Nursing
- Bethune-Cookman University College of Nursing & Health Science
- Albany State University Department of Nursing
- Grambling State University School of Nursing
- Southern University and A&M College School of Nursing
- Alcorn State University School of Nursing
- Lincoln University (MO) School of Nursing
- Prairie View A&M University College of Nursing
- Hampton University School of Nursing
- Howard University College of Nursing and Allied Health Sciences

**Top HBCU Nursing Programs Ranked by Nurse Journal:**
- Florida A&M University School of Nursing
- Oakwood University Department of Nursing
- Delaware State University Department of Nursing
- Winston-Salem State University Nursing BSN

　　　　　Mychal Wynn

- Dillard University College of Nursing
- Claflin University Department of Nursing
- Coahoma Community College Associate Degree Nursing (ADN)
- University of Arkansas at Pine Bluff Department of Nursing

RegisteredNursing.org provides one of the more comprehensive listings of HBCU nursing programs by state. HBCUConnect.com ranks the following as the best HBCU Nursing Schools:

- Hampton University School of Nursing
- North Carolina A&T State University School of Nursing
- Florida A&M University School of Nursing
- Alcorn State University School of Nursing
- Fayetteville State University School of Nursing
- Prairie View A&M University College of Nursing
- Winston-Salem State University Nursing BSN
- Coppin State University Nursing BSN
- Kentucky State University School of Nursing and Health Sciences
- Bowie State University Department of Nursing
- Morgan State University Department of Nursing
- Norfolk State University Bachelor Science in Nursing (BSN)
- Delaware State University Department of Nursing
- Hampton University School of Nursing
- Southern University and A&M College School of Nursing

Nursing programs are not only competitive to gain admission to the lower level program, even if you are admitted into the program, you are not guaranteed admission to the upper level program:

Acceptance into the nursing program is based upon the admission criteria. Meeting the minimal admission criteria does not guarantee admission into the Upper Division of Nursing. Based on the competitive nature of the program, some qualified applicants may not be admitted. A ranking system will be used to determine admission to the Division of Nursing. The ranking system awards points for each admission criterion. Please review information below and follow the guidelines explicitly to facilitate the processing of your application. Failure to comply with all directions and requirements will result in the application not being reviewed. [Winston-Salem State]

The Howard University College of Nursing Lower Level Curriculum is a 60 credit hour program. Acceptance into the upper level program is not guaranteed. However, if accepted into the Howard University College of Nursing and Allied Health Sciences Upper Division, you will be required to complete an additional 60 credit hour program.

**HBCU Nursing School Pathways**

The guaranteed early acceptance/assurance pathways through HBCUs into nursing school allows opportunities to plan your way into nursing school.

**Edward Waters University — University of Florida College of Nursing:** Allows up to five students from EWU to join the UF College of Nursing's Accelerated BSN program at the UF Health Jacksonville campus. The partnership gives qualified biological sciences majors the option of pursuing a nursing degree at UF's Jacksonville campus.

**Fisk University — Galen College of Nursing:** The Dual Track Degree Progression Option allowed for a seamless transition from earning a Bachelor of Arts (BA) or Bachelor of Science (BS) degree into Galen's Bachelor of Science in Nursing (BSN).

**Spelman College — Augusta University:** Augusta University's College of Nursing offers two pathways to the Master of Science in Nursing degree with a concentration in Clinical Nurse Leader. The first pathway is an innovative, accelerated graduate program for individuals with non-nursing bachelor's degrees. The second pathway is a bridge program to the Master of Science in Nursing degree for individuals who currently hold a Bachelor's degree in Nursing.

**Spelman College — Emory University Nell Hodgson Woodruff School of Nursing:** Emory University School of Nursing offers two pathways to obtain an entry level nursing degree. Students may consider the Dual Degree Nursing option or the Accelerated BSN/MSN option. Students from all majors may apply.

**Spelman College — University of Rochester Accelerated Bachelor's Program for Non-Nurses:** For applicants that already have a bachelor's degree, but are ready to make a career change. In just 12 months, you can earn a fully accredited nursing degree. The UR School of Nursing is one of the most respected nursing schools in the country.

**Tougaloo College — University of Mississippi Medical Center (UMMC):** Allows freshmen pre-nursing students to be accepted into the UMMC nursing school as a freshman and secure a spot and to avoid the competitive selection process as a sophomore/junior. This is offered annually to outstanding high school seniors and freshmen. Applicants who wish to be considered for early entry status must have an ACT score of 25; Cumulative high school GPA of 3.5; College GPA of 3.0 when accepted into the program and completion of all prerequisites with a grade of "C" or higher.

**Xavier University of Louisiana — Rush University College of Nursing:** The Preferential Admission Program whereby Rush will offer admission into the Master's Entry in Nursing (MSN) for Non-Nurses: Clinical Nurse Leader Program for up to 2 (two) qualified Xavier applicants for entry in the fall and up to two (2) qualified Xavier applicants for entry in the spring. The program prepares students for nursing leadership roles and advanced education in nursing (e.g., nurse practitioner, nurse anesthesia, etc.).

The College of Nursing has dedicated financial need and merit scholarships for diverse and underrepresented students in nursing. Students will be eligible for diversity scholarships if they are Black or African-American, Hispanic, American Indian or Alaska Native, specific Asian populations or male (groups underrepresented in nursing) or from financially disadvantaged backgrounds.

## Additional Considerations

**Naval Reserve Officers Training Corps (NROTC) – Nurse Option:**
A scholarship program that provides full tuition, monthly stipends, and summer training. Available to students interested in pursuing Bachelor of Science degree in nursing (BSN):

- Available only at a university that has a Navy ROTC affiliation and offers a state approved and Commission on Collegiate Nursing Education (CCNE) or Accreditation Commission for Education in Nursing (ACEN) accredited bachelor's degree in nursing program.

- If selected for scholarship, the selectee must major in a nursing degree program leading to BSN.

- On graduation, Nurse Option midshipmen are commissioned as regular officers in the Navy Nurse Corps.

- While in the program, male and female students participate in Navy ROTC and are referred to as midshipmen.

## HBCUs with the Navy Nurse Option:

- Southern University and A&M College

- Dillard University (affiliated with Tulane University)

- Howard University (Capital Battalion)

**Navy Nurse Candidate Program (NCP):** The NCP provides a monthly stipend for full-time juniors and/or seniors in accredited Bachelor of Science Nursing programs accredited by the Commission on Collegiate Nursing Education (CCNE) or the National League for Nursing Accrediting Commission, Inc (NLNAC). Students can apply for the NCP after their sophomore year.

- NCP participants may receive a substantial sign-on bonus paid in (2) installments and a monthly (taxable) stipend paid in (2) increments on the 1st and the 15th of each month for 24 months while in the program and which stops on the graduation date. No further funds are paid until you report for active duty.

- NCP participants are NOT entitled to tuition payments, reimbursement for books, fees, equipment, etc., or annual training. **This is not ROTC; no drill time is involved. **

- After graduation, participants attend (5) weeks of Officer Basic Training to become Navy Nurse Corps Officers. Service obligations depend on the length of the benefit received, generally 4 years of service for 12 months of scholarship or 5 years for 13 to 24 months of scholarship.

## Resources

As you develop your list of HBCU nursing programs, look beyond the college to the broad range of nursing pathways, such as:

- National Institutes of Health Clinical Center
- National Institutes of Health Clinical Research Nursing Residency Program
- U.S. Public Health Services Commissioned Corps
- Discover the Top 30 HBCU Nursing Programs in the U.S.

Governing bodies, boards, associations, accreditation, and networking organizations for nursing:

- Accreditation Commission for Education in Nursing (ACEN)
- American Association of Colleges of Nursing
- American Association of Nurse Practitioners
- American Nurses Association
- American Nurses Credentialing Center
- American Nurses Foundation
- American Society of Registered Nurses
- Black Nurses Coalition
- Black Nurses Matter
- Black Nurses Rock
- Council for Higher Education Accreditation
- Commission on Collegiate Nursing Education (CCNE)
- Equality for Nurses
- National Association of Healthcare Assistants
- National Association of Licensed Practical Nurses

- National Black Nurses Association
- National Coalition of Ethnic Minority Nurse Associations
- National Council of State Boards of Nursing (NCSBN)
- National Nurses United
- Registered Nursing

See NurseJournal for a comprehensive listing of local, state, and national nurses associations.

# HBCU Optometry Pathways

The following tables reflects information collected from the U.S. Bureau of Labor Statistics Occupational Outlook Handbook, *"Optometrists,"* and the Indeed Career Guide pertaining to related careers.

| Career | Salary | Description |
| --- | --- | --- |
| Optometrists | $145,632 | Optometrists diagnose, manage, and treat conditions and diseases of the human eye and visual system, including examining eyes and prescribing corrective lenses. Optometrists typically need a Doctor of Optometry (O.D.) degree, which takes 4 years of graduate-level study to complete. Every state requires optometrists to be licensed |
| Ophthalmologists | $216,410 | Physicians and surgeons diagnose and treat injuries or illnesses and address health maintenance. |
| Glaucoma Specialists | $380,00 | Glaucoma specialists diagnose glaucoma, an eye condition that damages the optic nerve. They examine patient eyes, create treatment plans and may perform surgery. Glaucoma specialists must follow the same educational path as other ophthalmologists. |

| Career | Salary | Description |
| --- | --- | --- |
| Ophthalmic Nurses | $71,358 | An ophthalmic nurse performs vision tests, gathers patient medical histories and helps with eye exams. They also administer medications and teach patients how to care for their eyes at home. Ophthalmic nurses are required to pass the National Council Licensure Examination for Registered Nurses (NCLEX-RN) to start practicing as a registered nurse. |
| Retinal Angiographers | $60,363 | A retinal angiographer helps ophthalmologists with clinical tasks, such as conducting eye exams and administering medications. They also teach patients how to use corrective lenses. Certified Retinal Angiographers (CRA's) are required to recertify at three-year intervals. |
| Ophthalmic Medical Technologists | $59,561 | An ophthalmic medical technologist helps an ophthalmologist with clinical tasks. They provide assistance during surgical procedures and maintain ophthalmic equipment. They also administer eye exams and eye medications, teach patients how to use corrective lenses and may train ophthalmic assistants and technicians. Clinical laboratory technologists and technicians typically need a bachelor's degree to enter the occupation. Technicians sometimes qualify for jobs with an associate's degree. Some states require technologists and technicians to be licensed. |

 Mychal Wynn

| Career | Salary | Description |
| --- | --- | --- |
| Certified Paraoptometric | $59,132 | A certified paraoptometric records patient medical histories, prepares patients for examinations and teaches them how to use contact lenses and eyeglasses. They may also provide vision therapy and educate patients on eye health. |
| Ophthalmic Scribes | $57,052 | An ophthalmic scribe documents communication between doctors and patients. They accompany physicians into an exam room to transcribe patient examinations and medical histories. |
| Opticians | $44.777 | Opticians may dispense or repair eyeglasses. Dispensing opticians sell eyeglasses and help patients find the right frames or contacts. In contrast, manufacturing opticians make and repair eyeglasses and ensure lenses fit into certain frames. Opticians typically need a high school diploma or the equivalent and receive on-the-job training. Some opticians enter the occupation with an associate's degree or a certificate in ophthalmic dispensing or a related field. |
| Certified Ophthalmic Technicians | $40,655 | A certified ophthalmic technician performs clinical tasks in addition to the duties of an ophthalmic assistant. They prepare patients to see an attending physician by taking their medical histories and performing various tests. They also prepare examination rooms, conduct vision screening examinations and administer medications as needed. |

| Career | Salary | Description |
|---|---|---|
| Optometric Technicians | $38,224 | An optometric technician's main responsibility is to assist an eye doctor in providing care to patients. Typically need at least a high school diploma or equivalent. They typically receive on-the-job training to attain competency. |
| Certified Paraoptometric Technicians | $35,245 | Administers diagnostic tests and medications. They use these tests to evaluate a patient's vision and eye muscle function. A certified ophthalmic assistant also sets up a room for procedures, gathers patient medical records, takes ocular measurements and teaches patients how to use contacts and eyeglasses. |
| Certified Ophthalmic Assistants | $32,958 | Administers diagnostic tests and medications. They use these tests to evaluate a patient's vision and eye muscle function. A certified ophthalmic assistant also sets up a room for procedures, gathers patient medical records, takes ocular measurements and teaches patients how to use contacts and eyeglasses. |

In the 2021 report by the American Optometric Association, *"Being Black in Optometry,"* several Black optometrists recount the challenges faced:

Dr. Devin Sasser, after graduating from Xavier University of Louisiana, attended the University of Missouri-St. Louis College of Optometry where he was the only Black in his 40-student class. "I had never been in an environment where I was the only Black man in the room. There's a level of community that you miss because of that. There's just no one who shares your cultural experience." He was able to connect with other Black optometry students by getting involved in the American Optometric Student Association (AOSA).



Mychal Wynn

Dr. Sherrol Reynolds, an associate professor and chief of the retina clinic at Nova Southern University College of Optometry recounts, "Did race impact my early experience? Of course, because you had some professors who treated certain demographics of students differently. You just felt that there were professors who had racist biases. I also experienced patients who did not want me as their doctor." For 15 years, Dr. Reynolds has been mentoring teenage girls at her former Broward County High School through a program called Women of Tomorrow. The majority of the school's students are Black. She meets with a group of girls once a month to talk about issues that affect women succeeding in the world. The program also offers the opportunity to receive college scholarships.

Dr. Jason Compton attended the State University of New York College of Optometry and recounts that in optometry school, and later in residency, he was the only Black man out of a class of about 70 students. Now, in his optometry practice he notes, "My patients love the fact that they're seeing a Black doctor." Sometimes when I get an older African American patient, they often acknowledge that they're so proud of me." He also speaks fluent Spanish, which helps reassure those patients whose first language is Spanish. "They feel very comfortable being able to communicate in their language about health care. Patients will feel more comfortable when they can open up, when they see someone who looks like them."

Whether pursuing a career as an ophthalmologist, optometrist, or optician, the American Academy of Ophthalmology provides important insight into choosing the right optometry pathway based on the level of education you are pursuing:

**Ophthalmologist (MD):** An ophthalmologist is a medical or osteopathic physician who specializes in eye and vision care. Ophthalmologist eye doctors differ from optometrists and opticians in their levels of training and in what they can diagnose and treat.

**Ophthalmic Nurse (RN):** An ophthalmic (or ophthalmology) nurse is a Registered Nurse who provides nursing care related to eye health and vision. Ophthalmic nurses work with ophthalmologists and other eye doctors to help patients who have eye conditions and diseases, such as cataracts, vision issues, astigmatism and eye injuries.

**Certified Ophthalmic Technician (COT):** A certified ophthalmic technician is a specially trained technician who assists an ophthalmologist with their patients' vision care, from routine eye exams to treating eye conditions. Depending on experience and certification, a COT can assist an optician with measurements and even work alongside an optometrist or ophthalmologist with tests and some small procedures leading up to prescription determination.

**Ophthalmic Technician:** An ophthalmic technician specializes in providing eye care services to patients under the supervision of an ophthalmologist. Among their responsibilities include conducting interviews, taking notes of the patients' symptoms, conducting eye examinations and tests, administering medication, and performing support tasks for ophthalmologists during procedures.

**Optometrist (OD):** An optometrist is not a medical doctor but is often referred to as an eye doctor because they hold a doctor of optometry (OD) degree.

**Optometric Technician:** An optometric technician works alongside Optometrists to provide comprehensive eye care to patients. They conduct preliminary testing, such as measuring visual acuity, before the Optometrist sees the patient. They also take and develop retinal photos, administer eye medications, instruct patients on how to use contact lenses and perform basic office duties. Optometric Technicians often specialize in a specific area of optometry, such as contact lenses, low vision, or pediatrics. They may also be certified to dispense eyeglasses and other vision devices.

**Optician:** An optician is an eyewear specialist who helps patients select the right type of glasses or contact lenses for their vision needs and facial features. They take precise measurements of patients' faces in order to create custom-fitted eyewear. Many Opticians also help patients adjust to their new glasses or contacts, and teach them how to properly care for their new eyewear. Opticians typically work in retail settings, such as optical stores, eyewear departments in department stores, or in private practices. Some Opticians may also work in hospitals or other healthcare facilities.

**Ophthalmic Photographer:** An ophthalmic photographer works with doctors on an ophthalmic medical team, taking photos of a patient's eye, including the retinas, corneas, and other ocular structures, to diagnose eye-related diseases and disorders and determine effective treatments or surgeries.

While it is difficult to identify how underrepresented Blacks are in all of the fields relating to ophthalmology, the BlackEyeCare Perspective is an organization designed and created to cultivate and foster lifelong relationships between Black eyecare professionals and the eyecare industry. Their industry partnerships and programming support their 13% Promise, a call for equity in eyecare through awareness, actionable change and accountability. They note that there is a shortage of optometrists and need for more diversity in eye care:

- 4.3% Black Optometry Students
- 3.2% Black Optometric Educators
- 2% Practicing Black Optometrists

There are no HBCUs among the 24 colleges of optometry. The Association of Schools and Colleges of Optometry reports that in 2023, there were 2,773 applicants to optometry school:

- 1204 White (45.76%)
- 883 Asian (32.35%)
- 361 Hispanic (11.24%)
- 134 Black (4.83%)

The acceptance rates of applicants by racial group show that Blacks submitted the fewest number of applications (134) and had the lowest percentage of acceptances (73):

- 77.0% Whites
- 74.3% Asians
- 63.1% Hispanics
- 54.4% Blacks

The percentage of students attending optometry school during 2023-24:

- 48.5% White
- 31.3% Asian
- 8.8% Hispanic/Latino
- 4.3% Black/African American

To increase the number of Black students entering optometry school, the National Optometric Association Mentorship Program sponsors an HBCU mentorship program. The objective of the program is to identify interested African American students at HBCUs and facilitate their professional development and career advancement in the field of Optometry. Eligible students must be in good academic standing-GPA minimum 3.0 or member of Pre-Health Program at an HBCU.

- The Poston Foundation ($1,000) and the NOA ($500) will provide a $1500 scholarship upon graduation to assist in admission preparation fees.
- The Poston Foundation ($1,000) and VSP Vision ($1,500) will provide a $2500 scholarship upon enrollment to aid in the purchase of first year equipment.
- NOA will support the attendance of 1-2 HBCU student(s) to one annual convention to network and meet minority optometrists.

Students selected in the 2023 mentorship cohort attended the following HBCUs:

- Bowie State University
- Fisk University
- Florida A&M University
- Howard University
- Miles College
- Spelman College
- Tennessee State University

- Prairie View A&M University
- Savannah State University

## Pathway to Becoming an Ophthalmologist

The American Academy of Ophthalmology notes that the pathway to becoming an ophthalmologist typically includes:

- A four-year college degree
- Four years of medical school
- One year post-graduate clinical internship, as outlined by the American Board of Ophthalmology
- Three year ophthalmology residency training program

After completing this lengthy education—a total of 12 to 14 years—ophthalmologists are licensed to practice medicine and surgery. Ophthalmologists are the only eye care providers with the appropriate levels of medical education and clinical training to safely perform delicate eye surgery. This advanced medical training allows ophthalmologists to diagnose and treat a wider range of conditions than optometrists and opticians.

Some ophthalmologists, referred to as subspecialists, specialize in a specific area of medical or surgical eye care. This usually requires one or two years of additional, more in-depth training (called a fellowship) in one of the main subspecialty areas such as Glaucoma, Retina, Cornea, Pediatrics, Neurology, Oculoplastic Surgery or others.

## Pathway to Becoming an Optometrist

Unlike ophthalmologists who attend 4 years of medical school, optometrists attend 4 years of optometry school. Optometrists may attend school for an additional year or more to be trained in a specialty, such as vision rehabilitation or vision therapy. The Association of Schools and Colleges of Optometry provides a listing of the 23 accredited optometry schools in the United States, one of which is in Puerto Rico. Board certification is received from the American Board of Optometry.

To qualify for admission to optometry school, your undergraduate coursework should typically include:

- Calculus
- Anatomy
- Physiology
- Organic Chemistry
- Biochemistry
- Microbiology
- Statistics
- Psychology
- 40 hours of shadowing

## Pathway to Becoming an Optician

Most opticians pursue formal training through either a certification program at a vocational school, or a two-year Associate Degree program in Ophthalmic Dispensing. Both of these options are available to students who have a high school diploma or GED.

In some cases, it is also possible to become an optician by participating in a two-year apprenticeship program with a practicing optician. This route consists of learning on-the-job skills without any formal classroom instruction. However, this is a less formalized path, and most employers prefer candidates who attended a certificate program or obtained an associate's degree.

## HBCU Optometry Pathways

The guaranteed early acceptance/assurance pathways through HBCUs into optometry school allows opportunities to plan your way into optometry school, which have lowest acceptance rates among general applicants.

**Hampton University — Pennsylvania College of Optometry at Salus University:** The Hampton University, Salus University Pennsylvania College of Optometry, 4+4 Doctor of Optometry Degree Program is offered collaboratively by both institutions. The program identifies juniors in the HU Pre-Health Program who have earned at least a 3.0 Grade Point Average (GPA) or above and score a 300+ score on the OAT (Optometry Admissions Test).

At Hampton University premedical students interested in obtaining doctoral degrees in medicine, dentistry, osteopathic medicine, podiatry, veterinary medicine, optometry, chiropractic, and public health/health care administration, should apply to become a member of the Pre-Health Program. Juniors, sophomores, and second-semester freshmen, who possess a minimum 3.0 GPA (Grade Point Average), are eligible for membership.

**North Carolina Central University — Illinois College of Optometry:** 3+4 program, where you will spend three years as an undergraduate and then join ICO for the next four years. In most cases, after your first year at ICO, you will have completed the requirements to receive a bachelor's degree from your undergraduate institution. After completing the next three years of successful coursework, you will graduate as a Doctor of Optometry.

**Spelman College — Nova Southeastern University College of Optometry:** The NSU Early Selection Program in Optometry (ESPO) provides qualified students with the opportunity for early acceptance into the NUS-COO OD Program.

**Resources**

Governing boards, associations, and networking organizations for ophthalmologists, optometrists, and opticians:

- American Academy of Ophthalmology
- American Association for Pediatric Ophthalmology and Strabismus
- American Board of Ophthalmology
- American Board of Optometry
- American Glaucoma Society
- American Ophthalmological Society
- American Optometric Association
- Association of Regulatory Boards of Optometry

- Commission on Opticianry Accreditation
- Contact Lens Society of America
- International Council of Ophthalmology
- National Academy of Opticianry
- National Board of Examiners in Optometry
- National Contact Lens Examiners
- National Eye Institute
- National Federation of Opticianry Schools
- National Optometric Association
- Optical Women's Association
- Society to Advance Opticianry
- The Vision Council
- United Opticians Association
- Vision of Hope Foundation

| **Black-owned Eyewear Brands** | |
|---|---|
| 3rd Eye View | GodNII |
| Anwuli Eyewear | Hyve Life |
| Bôhten | Kimeze |
| Bon Vivant Safety Eyewear | Liberated Eyewear |
| CEV Collection | Savoir Faire |
| Dani Joh Eyewear | Shades of Shade |
| Ember Niche | SWAV Eyewear |
| Eyewear Love Affair | Vontélle |

# HBCU Pharmacy Pathways

There are many levels to pursue a career in pharmaceutical sciences, which provides options during each level of your education. Reflected in the tables is data collected from the Occupational Outlook Handbook, *"Pharmacy Occupations,"* and from the Indeed Career Guide pertaining to related careers.

| Career | Salary | Description |
|---|---|---|
| Director of Pharmacy | $147,235 | A director of a pharmacy is responsible for overseeing a pharmacy's operations and management. They procure and store medications and work in coordination with medical staff to dispense them safely to patients. |
| Pharmacists | $136,030 | Pharmacists dispense prescription medications and provide information to patients about the drugs and their use. Typically need a Doctor of Pharmacy (PharmD) degree. Every state requires pharmacists to be licensed. |
| Clinical Pharmacists | $125,318 | A clinical pharmacist works in cooperation with physicians and other clinical health providers to review and dispense medications to patients. Most places that hire clinical pharmacists require them to have a doctorate degree in pharmacy. |

| Career | Salary | Description |
| --- | --- | --- |
| Oncology Pharmacists | $119,755 | An oncology pharmacist prepares and dispenses chemotherapy drugs used in cancer treatments. They assess the quality of these drugs and make their review available to cancer hospitals and cancer treatment centers. Oncology pharmacists provide evidence-based and patient-centered care by pharmacists who are specialized and certified in oncology in conjunction with other disciplines to further advance patient care. |
| Long-term Care Pharmacists | $119,755 | A long-term care pharmacist oversees pharmaceutical services for patients in a long-term care facility. |
| Nuclear Pharmacists | $119,755 | A nuclear pharmacist is responsible for preparing, testing and dispensing radiopharmaceuticals for diagnosing and treating different types of cancers and many other diseases. |
| Pharmacologists | $110,136 | A pharmacologist is a medical scientist who works with hospitals, biopharmaceutical companies and other organizations to discover and develop therapies to treat cancer and various other diseases. |
| Pharmacy Technicians | $40,300 | Pharmacy technicians help pharmacists dispense prescription medication to customers or health professionals. Pharmacy technicians usually need a high school diploma or equivalent and learn their duties through on-the-job training, or they may complete a postsecondary education program in pharmacy technology. Most states regulate pharmacy technicians, which is a process that may require passing an exam or completing a formal education or training program. |

Other pharmacy-related careers include: Pharmaceutical Research Technician; Laboratory Technician; Medical Science Liaison Clinical Research Coordinator; Medical Writer; Pharmaceutical Sales Rep; Medical Rep; Clinical Research Associate; Research Scientist; Clinical Research Scientist; Pharmacologist Veterinary Pharmacist; and Toxicologist.

Aisha Morris Moultry's research, *"The Evolving Role of Historically Black Pharmacy Schools in a Changing Environment,"* notes that there are 6,704 Black students out of the 60,594 students attending pharmacy school in the U.S. (11 percent). 1,080 (16 percent) Black pharmacy students attend an HBCU School of Pharmacy. Even with Black students choosing to attend an HBCU School of Pharmacy, the average Black enrollment at HBCU pharmacy schools varies between 19 - 27 percent of student enrollment.

The National Center for Health Workforce Analysis, *"State of the U.S. Health Care Workforce, 2023,"* reports the following racial breakdown among pharmacists.

| Race/Ethnicity | Pharmacist Workforce | U.S. Population |
|---|---|---|
| Asian, Non-Hispanic | 21.0% | 6% |
| Black, Non-Hispanic | 6.5% | 12.4% |
| Hispanic | 4.9% | 18% |
| White | 64.8% | 59% |
| Other or Multi-racial | 2.6% | 4% |

Rather than waiting until the end of your undergraduate program to research pharmacy schools, it would be prudent to research undergraduate through pharmacy school pathways to maximize your college and scholarship options. For example, the University of Maryland Eastern Shore describes their School of Pharmacy and Health Professions as:

> The School of Pharmacy and Health Professions consists of five academic departments: Kinesiology, Pharmacy, Physical Therapy, Physician Assistant and Rehabilitation Services. Undergraduate programs include Exercise Science and Rehabilitation Services. Graduate programs include the master's degree in Physician Assistant studies and Rehabilitation Counseling, the Doctor of Physical Therapy

(DPT), and the Doctor of Pharmacy (PharmD) as well as Pharmaceutical Science (PhD). Students are actively involved with faculty initiatives to improve the health and well-being of the community through health education/promotion. A variety of internship sites for student practical experiences are available.

The Howard University College Pharmacy describes their programs as:

At HUCOP, we emphasize the power of teamwork. Our college community, composed of our dedicated faculty, staff, proud alumni, preceptors, board of visitors and generous supporters champions the values of Collaboration, Accountability, Respect, and Excellence (C.A.R.E.) as the cornerstones of our success.

Howard offers BS/PharmD; 4-year entry level PharmD; 5-year PharmD/ MBA; MS and PhD in Pharmaceutical Sciences; Non-Traditional Doctor of Pharmacy; and AA/PharmD programs.

Florida A&M College of Pharmacy & Pharmaceutical Sciences, Institute of Public Health describes their program as:

The Florida A&M University College of Pharmacy and Pharmaceutical Sciences, Institute of Public Health program offers its learners PharmD, BS, MS, PhD, MPH and DrPH degrees. With its main campus in Tallahassee, Florida, it is the only pharmacy program in the United States with a fully accredited Institute of Public Health. The College has additional practice centers in Jacksonville, Davie, and Tampa with a campus in Crestview, which support the infrastructure for the College's statewide commitment to pharmacy and public health education through research, teaching, and community service.

Florida A&M notes the following achievements:

- Graduate over 20 percent of the nation's African American pharmacists

- Enroll the largest number and percentage of African Americans in the PharmD program

- Graduate over 60 percent of the African American PhD recipients in the four areas of the pharmaceutical sciences

- Enroll the largest number and the largest percentage of African Americans pursuing a PhD in one of the pharmaceutical sciences

- Become the first institution in the State of Florida to offer the Doctor of Public Health (DrPH) degree program

- Enroll the largest number of African Americans pursuing the DrPH degree in Florida A&M University

- Develop state-of-the-art pharmacy technology to support PharmD, PhD, and DrPH programs

- Acquire state-of-the-art research equipment to provide training to PharmD, PhD, and DrPH learners

- Achieve the first scholarship endowment by the pharmacy alumni association to support minority learners

With other HBCU Schools of Pharmacy offering various programs of study, the more you know about the programs, communities in which you would be living for 6 - 10 years of more through your undergraduate and graduate studies, and the students and professors with whom you will be working, the more capable you will be for choosing the right educational and professional pathway.

National Library of Medicine's *"2021 National healthcare Quality and Disparities Report,"* notes the percentage of pharmacists by racial group in the U.S.:

- 65% White

- 20% Asian

- 7% Black

- 5% Hispanic

2019 enrollment at HBCU pharmacy schools:

- 248 - Howard University College of Pharmacy

- 468 - Florida A&M University College of Pharmacy & Pharmaceutical Sciences, Institute of Public Health

- 141 - Hampton University School of Pharmacy

- 321 - Texas Southern University College of Pharmacy & Health Sciences

- 142 - University of Maryland Eastern Shore School of

Pharmacy and Health Professions

- 608 - Xavier University of Louisiana College of Pharmacy

Xavier University of Louisiana, founded by Saint Katharine Drexel and the Sisters of the Blessed Sacrament, is Catholic. The mission of the College of Pharmacy's health sciences programs is to prepare students to become outstanding leaders as healthcare providers and scientists to impact the medically underserved, particularly African American communities, to achieve health equity, eliminate disparities and improve the health of all populations through patient-centered care, community engagement, and research or other scholarly work.

The Xavier University of Louisiana College of Pharmacy is one of the top 4 Colleges of Pharmacy in the U.S. for graduating Africans Americans with Doctor of Pharmacy Degrees. Students wishing to pursue a Doctor of Pharmacy (PharmD) degree through Xavier's College of Pharmacy must complete 57 credit hours of pre-requisite courses prior to being admitted to the PharmD program. The pre-pharmacy requirements may be completed at Xavier University or any accredited university.

## HBCU Pharmacy School Pathways

The guaranteed early acceptance/assurance pathways through HBCUs into pharmacy school allows opportunities to plan your way into pharmacy school.

**Howard University College of Pharmacy:** This program allows students to gain their BS and PharmD. Degrees in 7 years. Students must complete the prerequisites and major in a listed major. Partner schools are:

- Alabama A&M University
- Cheyney University
- Bennett College
- Fayetteville State University
- Fort Valley State University
- Howard University

                    Mychal Wynn

- Johnson C. Smith University
- Lincoln University
- North Carolina Central University
- Tuskegee University
- Virginia State University

**North Carolina A&T — UNC Eshelman School of Pharmacy:** Early Assurance Program (EAP). This partnership means current NC A&T students interested in pursuing a doctoral degree in pharmacy may be eligible for assured admission.

**Tougaloo College — University of Mississippi Pharmacy School:** Preferred Admission agreement. Interested freshmen may apply to the program during their second semester at Tougaloo. Successful applicants will have a GPA of 3.25 or above in required pre-pharmacy courses (Biology 111, Chemistry 115/117, Math 103 or above) with no grades below C, as well as evidence of volunteer experience. In successive years identified students must continue to achieve at this level in required coursework. Seniors must have a PCAT score of 400 and a writing score of 3.0. Students who achieve at this level will be automatically admitted to the Ole Miss Pharmacy School.

**Tougaloo College — Xavier University of Louisiana School of Pharmacy:** Dual degree in pharmacy. Students will be identified for early acceptance into the Pharmacy School during their sophomore year at Tougaloo College. Students who are accepted will be required to meet the guidelines of the program prior to their transfer to Xavier after their junior year at Tougaloo. On successful completion of the first year of pharmacy school Tougaloo will accept Xavier courses toward the completion of a Tougaloo science major and BS degree. Students must maintain a GPA of 2.75 or above.

**Tuskegee University — Auburn University Harrison College of Pharmacy:** This agreement establishes an Early Acceptance Program (EAP) to highly qualified individuals admitted as undergraduate students to Auburn University or Tuskegee University. Further information may be obtained from the School's Website or Office of Academic and Student Affairs. Prerequisite Requirements.

**Tuskegee University — Lake Erie School of Pharmacy:** Early Acceptance Program (EAP) establishes an EAP pursuant to which Tuskegee University undergraduate students are enrolled simultaneously by Tuskegee University and by LECOM as participants in EAP. The EAP is designed to facilitate the admission of Tuskegee University students into LECOM's Doctor of Pharmacy program. LECOM will interview qualified students prior to their enrollment at Tuskegee University or within the first two years of study at Tuskegee University. Students interviewing successfully will be offered a provisional acceptance to LECOM's Doctor of Pharmacy program.

## Resources

Boards, associations, and networking organizations for pharmacists:

- Accreditation Council for Pharmacy Education
- American Association of Colleges of Pharmacy
- American Association of Pharmaceutical Scientists
- American Association of Pharmacy Technicians
- American College of Clinical Pharmacy
- American Pharmacists Association
- American Society of Health-System Pharmacists
- Association of Black Health System Pharmacists
- Black Pharma
- Black Pharmacy Students' Association
- Black Women Pharmacists
- Board of Pharmacy Specialties
- Hematology/Oncology Pharmacy Association
- Minority Women Pharmacists Association
- National Alliance of State Pharmacy Associations

- National Association of Boards of Pharmacy

- National Community Pharmacists Association

- National Pharmaceutical Association

- National Pharmaceutical Council

- National Pharmacy Technician Association

- Schools and Colleges of Pharmacy

- Society of Infectious Diseases Pharmacists

- Student National Pharmaceutical Association

- U.S. Pharmacist

- U.S. Pharmacopeia

- Young Black Pharma

# HBCU Physical Therapy Pathways

Reflected in the tables is information collected from the Occupational Outlook Handbook, *"Physical Therapists,"* regarding physical therapists and related careers.

| Career | Salary | Description |
| --- | --- | --- |
| Physical Therapists | $99,710 | Physical therapists help injured or ill people improve movement and manage pain. Physical therapists entering the occupation need a Doctor of Physical Therapy (DPT) degree. All states require physical therapists to be licensed. |
| Occupational Therapists | $96,370 | Occupational therapists evaluate and treat people who have injuries, illnesses, or disabilities to help them with vocational, daily living, and other skills that promote independence. Typically need a master's degree in occupational therapy. All states require occupational therapists to be licensed. |
| Certified Lymphedema Therapists | $85,000 | Certification in Decongestive Therapy (CDT) and the management of lymphedema affecting a variety of peripheral body parts - upper and lower extremities. |

| Career | Salary | Description |
| --- | --- | --- |
| Physical Therapist Assistants | $58,740 | Physical therapist assistants and aides are supervised by physical therapists to help patients regain movement and manage pain after injuries and illnesses. Physical therapist assistants entering the occupation typically need an associate's degree from an accredited program and a license or certification. Physical therapist aides usually need a high school diploma or equivalent and on-the-job training. |
| Athletic Trainers | $57,930 | Athletic trainers specialize in preventing, diagnosing, and treating muscle and bone injuries and illnesses. Typically need at least a bachelor's degree, and master's degrees are common. Nearly all states require athletic trainers to have a license or certification; requirements vary by state. |
| Recreational Therapists | $57,120 | Recreational therapists plan, direct, and coordinate recreation-based medical treatment programs for people with disabilities, injuries, or illnesses. Recreational therapists typically need a bachelor's degree to enter the occupation. Many employers require them to be certified. |
| Exercise Physiologists | $54,860 | Exercise physiologists develop fitness and exercise programs to help people improve their health. Typically need a bachelor's degree in exercise science, exercise physiology, or a related field to enter the occupation. |

The American Physical Therapy Association's, *"APTA Physical Therapy Workforce Analysis,"* provides the percentage of physical therapists and physical therapist assistants by racial group.

| Physical Therapists | Physical Therapist Assistants |
| --- | --- |
| 84.3% White | 73.8% White |
| 6.9% Asian | 11.8% Hispanic |
| 3.5% Hispanic | 7.0% Asian |
| 2.5% Black | 5.8% Black |

The American Board of Physical Therapy Residency & Fellowship Education reports the number and percentage of physical therapists in the 2020 graduating class receiving residencies and fellowships by racial group.

| Residencies | Fellowships |
| --- | --- |
| 511 (64.8%) White | 108 (65.1%) White |
| 48 (6.1%) Asian | 25 (15.1%) Asian |
| 36 (4.7%) Hispanic | 10 (6.0%) Hispanic |
| 31 (3.9%) Black | 4 (2.4%) Black |

The Commission on Accreditation in Physical Therapy Education reports that in 2021, there were 3,322 faculty positions at schools with DPT programs. The table below shows the representation of DPT faculty by racial group.

| Race | Number of Faculty | Percentage |
| --- | --- | --- |
| White | 2,784 | 83.8% |
| Asian | 231 | 7.0% |
| Hispanic | 130 | 4.0% |
| Black | 101 | 3.0% |

Achieving equitable representation in physical therapy has been a long fought battle. Mary McKinney Edmonds, founder of the Cleveland State University physical therapy program, recounts in a 1998 interview: (APTA, 2022)

> On the "Jim Crow train" that she and other Black college students rode from northern states to HBCUs in the South:



Mychal Wynn

*"The Blacks had to go into these bad train cars that were right next to —
at that time they fired up with coal, and the cinders would blow into the
first car and that's where they put us. And so, going to Atlanta — that's
where the culture shock was. But when you talk about the resiliency of
Blacks — students coming on that train from Chicago, Indianapolis,
Detroit, Cleveland, Pittsburgh, all met there. And we were all in these
trains together, so we developed our own little groups of friends …
coming home at Christmas we would sing the whole way up, and it was,
you know, we were in a bad system, but there were always ways you
could make it at least palatable."*

On the challenges of clinical affiliations for Black PT students in the
1950s:

*"When we wanted to go on our affiliations, there were some places
where we could work in the clinics, but we couldn't live in the dorm. I
won't mention them. So we had to choose places in the north."*

On creating pathways for more PTs from minority populations:

*"We need to get down in the elementary schools to try to get more
minority physical therapists. How you do that is to get them motivated
really early and keep them from being shuffled into vocational programs
and programs that are not going to get them there, and also to get into
the community colleges and get them on the proper tracks."*

The National Association of Black Physical Therapists is forging
a community among Black physical therapists and supports the
Black Academicians in Physical Therapy program. The eight-month
career development program is offered by the National Association
of Black Physical Therapists, providing resources, mentorship,
and support. Joining in this collaboration is the Coalition of Black
Physical Therapists Facebook Group.

Becoming a physical therapist takes six to seven years and requires
a bachelor's degree in a related field, a Doctor of Physical Therapy
(DPT), and state licensure. The University of St. Augustine for Health
Sciences lists the *"5 Best Physical therapy Programs & Undergraduate
Degrees in 2024"* as:

- **Kinesiology:** While biology explores the science of life in
  general, kinesiology hones in on the dynamics of human
  movement. Because the field is closely related to physical

therapy, many students find it to be a natural stepping stone into the best DPT programs.

- **Exercise Science:** Because activity-related injuries are one of the most common reasons why people see physical therapists, exercise science is an ideal major if you're applying to one of the top physical therapy programs.

- **Health Science:** Students studying health science will gain a broad understanding of the health sector. Health Science majors gain insights into the determinants of health and disease, which can prepare them for the holistic approach required in physical therapy.

- **Biology:** Physical therapy requires knowledge of the human body, so it should be no surprise that biology is one of the best degrees to pursue before applying to any physical therapy programs. Biology students explore the science of life in a broad sense, tapping into the inner workings of various living organisms—all of which can provide insight into health and wellness.

- **Psychology:** Gaining an understanding of human psychology provides insight into the motivations behind an individual's actions, a crucial competency for applicants to physical therapy programs. The study of human movement, behavior, and response forms a vital component of PT education, offering extensive benefits.

In 1974, Howard University created the first physical therapy department at an HBCU as part of the College of Nursing and Allied Health Sciences. The Physical Therapy program offers an accredited program leading to a Doctor of Physical Therapy (DPT) degree. Students in this program are exposed to cutting edge research and practice in both the classroom and the clinic.

**Program Outcomes**

**Class of 2022**

- Licensure Rate - First Attempt NPTE Pass Rate - (4/4) 100%
- Licensure Rate - Ultimate NPTE Pass Rate - (4/4) 100%
- Graduation Rate - 93%
- Employment Rate (for licensed physical therapists) - 100%

**Class of 2023**

- Licensure Rate - First Attempt NPTE Pass Rate - (17/21) 81%
- Licensure Rate - Ultimate NPTE Pass Rate - (19/21) 91%
- Graduation Rate - 88%
- Employment Rate (for licensed physical therapists) - 100%

When considering undergraduate majors in planning a pathway into becoming a Doctor of Physical Therapy, it is wise to consider what your career options would be if you change your mind. Would you enjoy a career as a physical therapy assistant or a career in exercise science of kinesiology? If you are passionate about your undergraduate major, you will have greater and more personally fulfilling career options.

The American Physical Therapy Association's PTMovesMe Campaign provides support materials for high school and college students, counselors, educators, and advisors interested in learning more about careers as a physical therapists or physical therapist assistant.

Currently, there are eight HBCUs offering Doctor of Physical Therapy programs:

- Alabama State University
- Florida A&M University
- Hampton University
- Howard University
- Langston University
- Tennessee State University

- University of Maryland Eastern Shore
- Winston-Salem State University

It is important to research each program. For example, the Doctor of Physical Therapy program at the University of Maryland Eastern Shore is an integrated 3-year curriculum of academic and clinical education.

- **Evidence-Based Curriculum:** The curriculum is infused with current physical therapy evidence. Students become comfortable with reading and applying research evidence pertinent to the practice of physical therapy.

- **Independent Study:** The independent study offers a means for students to pursue both academic and clinical interests beyond the scope of course work in the program under the direction of a faculty adviser.

- **Research Project:** Students successfully complete a research project with a partner(s) and under the advisement of a faculty member.

Winston-Salem State University offers an early assurance program for WSSU students:

Earn your BS in Exercise Science from WSSU to get a leg up on the competition when you apply to the University's highly-competitive Doctor of Physical Therapy (DPT) program. WSSU's DPT program receives well over 600 applications for 28 seats in the program. The early assurance agreement is a significant advantage for WSSU undergraduates.

LaDonna Dingle, PT, who works with oncology patients as a Certified Lymphedema Therapist, notes the impact of attending an HBCU on her career as a physical therapist in the American Physical Therapy Association's article, *"HBCU DPT Programs Produce Great PTs: It Shouldn't Be a Secret."*

In the fall of 1992, I entered Spelman College in Atlanta, one of two HBCUs for women in the United States. Our professors and faculty encouraged us to be leaders in our chosen courses of study and helped us to become what they called "women who change the world." There was nothing we could not accomplish because of our race or gender, and Spelman prepared us to make a difference in the world.

Prior to entering the program [PT Program at the University of Maryland - Eastern Shore], I assumed that as students in an HBCU most of my classmates would be African American, but that was not the case. Although the undergraduate student population at UMES was primarily African American, the student population of the graduate program in physical therapy was not. In fact, in my graduating class of approximately 24 students, only two of us were African American.

## Physical Therapy Assistant

Physical therapist assistants are licensed to provide care under the direction and supervision of a licensed physical therapist. The American Physical Therapy Association reports that 72 percent of physical therapist assistants work in hospitals or privately-owned (outpatient) physical therapy practices. A typical PTA program is 2 years covering such areas as:

- Anatomy

- Physiology

- Exercise Physiology

- Biomechanics

- Kinesiology

- Neuroscience

- Clinical Pathology

- Behavioral Sciences

- Communication

- Ethics/Values

## Physical Therapist Assistant Program

Nearly all physical therapist assistant programs are offered by community colleges and technical schools. Albany State University is the only HBCU offering a Physical Therapist Assistant Associate of Science degree program. After successful completion of the four semester PTA program, this includes both didactic and clinical components; an Associate of Science degree will be awarded. Graduates will be academically eligible to apply for national licensure by examination through the Georgia State Board of Physical Therapy.

When applying to a physical therapy school, you may apply to multiple physical therapist education programs through one application submitted through the Physical Therapist Centralized Application Service (PTCAS). There are over 300 accredited Doctor of Physical Therapy (DPT) Programs, including the 8 HBCUs previously noted.

**HBCU Physical Therapist Pathways**

**Spelman College — Auburn University School of Kinesiology:** The Future Scholars Summer Research Bridge Program aids in the recruitment and transition of junior and senior-level undergraduates from traditionally underrepresented groups into Auburn's School of Kinesiology graduate programs.

**Xavier University of Louisiana — University of Southern California (USC PT):** The Division of Biokinesiology and Physical Therapy at the University of Southern California (USC PT) and Xavier University of Louisiana (XULA) have established an Early Assurance Program (EAP) to advance the success of students who desire to attend and complete physical therapy school and enter the physical therapy profession in order to contribute as leaders in the physical therapy workforce. It is a competitive program offered to students at XULA in their sophomore year who are committed to a career in physical therapy. The EAP is designed for students who wish to make the most of their undergraduate experience without having to apply to multiple schools in their final year of college. The collaboration offers an opportunity for students to develop skills in their preparation for physical therapy school through junior summer experiences and interactions with USC PT faculty and staff. USC PT seeks applicants who will benefit from these experiences and who will add to our community of learners through the diversity of their background and experiences.

The program outlines the academic qualifications so that a high school student, community college student, or current college student is aware of the program criteria:

- Academically qualified students who have a cumulative GPA of 3.2 or higher and a science GPA of 3.2 or higher at the end of their sophomore year (spring semester) may apply to the USC PT EAP. Classes that are included in science GPA are:

    - **Biological Sciences:** General Biology I & II, Anatomy, & Physiology

    - **Chemistry:** General Chemistry I & II, Biochemistry I & II (if taken instead of or as a supplement to General Chemistry)

    - **Physics:** General Physics I & II

- If accepted via EAP, students will be required to take the GRE and submit official scores to USC before they enroll. It is recommended that EAP accepted students prepare to take the GRE as early as the summer after junior year (e.g. June-July) but no later than the end of the fall semester of senior year (December). GRE scores will be used primarily for advising and course placement.

With a 3-year cost of over $230,000, it is advisable that you begin researching scholarships and graduate fellowships as soon as you decide that this is the career pathway that you want to pursue.

**Resources**

Boards, associations, and physical therapy networking organizations:

- Academy of Lymphatic Studies

- Academy of Pediatric Physical Therapy

- Accreditation Council for Occupational Therapy Education

- Accredited PT and PTA Programs

- American Academy of Physical Therapy

- American Academy of Orthopaedic Manual Physical

- American Board of Physical Therapy Residency & Fellowship Education

- American Board of Physical Therapy Specialists

- American Council of Academic Physical Therapy

- American Occupational Therapy Association

- American Occupational Therapy Foundation

- American Physical Therapy Association

- Coalition of Occupational Therapy Advocates for Diversity

- Federation of State Boards of Physical Therapy

- Lymphology Association of North America

- National Association of Advisors for the Health Professions

- National Association of Black Physical Therapists

- National Board for Certification in Occupational Therapy

- Physical Therapists Residency and Fellowship Programs

- Physical Therapy Centralized Application Service

- U.S. Department of Veterans Affairs Physical Therapy Residency Program

# HBCU Podiatry Pathways

The following table reflects information collected from Salary.com regarding podiatrists and related careers.

| Career | Salary | Description |
| --- | --- | --- |
| Podiatrists | $141,650 | Podiatrists provide medical and surgical care for people with foot, ankle, and lower leg problems. Podiatrists must earn a Doctor of Podiatric Medicine (DPM) degree and complete a 3-year residency program. Every state requires podiatrists to be licensed. |
| Podiatry Office Managers | $86,337 | Podiatrists must stay up-to-date with the latest advances in technology, regulations, and best practices to ensure their practices remain competitive and provide the highest level of patient care. Podiatry managers manage a podiatrist practice. |
| Podiatry Nurses | $75,412 | Nurses, (including DNP, NP, BSN, RN, LPN/LVN) who have certification in providing "routine foot care" in a podiatry practice. |
| Podiatry Medical Assistants | $44,085 | Podiatry medical assistants have the skills and knowledge needed to work with a podiatrist in his or her practice. Podiatrists are doctors of podiatric medicine who specialize in treating conditions that affect the feet and ankles. Most medical assistants in podiatry have completed formal education in a medical assisting program. One-year certificate/diploma programs and two-year associate degree programs are available in medical assisting. |

Podiatrists are doctors of podiatric medicine (D.P.M.) specializing in diagnosing and treating the foot, ankle, and lower leg. Podiatrists attend podiatric medical school, typically for 4 years. Some of the areas of treatment include screening for diabetic foot complications, foot exams, and education on proper foot care practices. Specializations include orthopedics, surgery and public health. Certified specialties include pediatrics, sports medicine, diabetic foot care, geriatrics, dermatology, and radiology.

The federal government recognizes podiatrists as physicians and that podiatric physicians' education and training are equivalent to the education and training of MDs and DOs. The APMA infographic compares the required training for Doctors of Podiatric Medicine (DPM), Doctors of Medicine (MD), and Doctors of Osteopathic Medicine (DO).

Podiatric physicians and surgeons receive basic and clinical science education and training comparable to that of allopathic and osteopathic physicians:

- four years of undergraduate education focusing on life sciences

- four years of graduate study in an accredited podiatric medical college

- at least three years of postgraduate, hospital-based residency training

According to research from Zippia, only 1.9 percent of podiatrists are Black, which is the lowest percentage since 2010.

**HBCU Podiatry School Pathways**

**Tuskegee University — Lake Erie College of Osteopathic Medicine**: This agreement establishes an Early Acceptance Program (EAP) pursuant to which Tuskegee University undergraduate students are enrolled simultaneously by Tuskegee University and by LECOM as participants in the EAP. LECOM has a School of Podiatric Medicine.

**Hampton University** is one of the few HBCUs listing podiatry as an area of premedical study.

 Mychal Wynn

**Resources**

Governing boards, associations, and podiatry networking organizations:

- Advancing foot and ankle medicine and surgery
- American Academy of Podiatric Sports Medicine
- American Association of Colleges of Podiatric Medicine
- American Association of Women Podiatrists
- American Board of Foot and Ankle Surgery
- American Board of Multiple Specialties in Podiatry
- American Board of Podiatric Medicine
- American Board of Podiatric Surgery
- American College of Foot and Ankle Pediatrics
- American College of Foot and Ankle Podiatric Medicine
- American College of Foot and Ankle Surgeons
- American College of Podiatric Medicine
- American Foot Care Nurses Association
- American Podiatric Medical Association
- American Podiatric Medical Students Association
- American Society of Podiatric Medical Assistants
- American Society of Podiatric Surgeons
- BlackDoctors.org
- Black Doctors USA
- Black Healthcare & Medical Association
- Council on Podiatric Medical Education
- Federation of Podiatric Medical Boards
- National Podiatric Medical Association
- Podiatric Medical Colleges
- Podiatric Medical Fellowships

# HBCU Veterinary Pathways

While *"HBCU Scholarships"* provides a comprehensive examination of scholarship opportunities unique to students attending HBCUs, if you are interested in studying pre-veterinary science, it is one of the fully funded disciplines under the 1890 National Scholars Program. The scholarship provides recipients with full tuition, fees, books, and room and board. Scholars attend one of the 19 1890 land-grant universities. The scholarship may also include work experience at USDA. The program is a crucial part of USDA's Next Generation efforts. The following tables reflects information collected from the Occupational Outlook Handbook, *"Veterinarians."*

| Career | Salary | Description |
| --- | --- | --- |
| Veterinarians | $119,100 | Veterinarians care for the health of animals and work to protect public health. Veterinarians must have a Doctor of Veterinary Medicine degree from an accredited veterinary college, as well as a state license. |
| Agricultural and Food Scientists | $76,400 | Agricultural and food scientists research ways to improve the efficiency and safety of agricultural establishments and products. Agricultural and food scientists need at least a bachelor's degree from an accredited postsecondary institution, although many get advanced degrees. |
| Zoologists and Wildlife Biologists | $70,600 | Zoologists and wildlife biologists study animals, those both in captivity and in the wild, and how they interact with their ecosystems. Zoologists and wildlife biologists typically need a bachelor's degree for entry-level positions and may need a master's degree for higher level jobs. |

| Career | Salary | Description |
| --- | --- | --- |
| Veterinary Technologists and Technicians | $43,740 | Veterinary technologists and technicians do medical tests that help diagnose animals' injuries and illnesses. Veterinary technologists and technicians must complete a postsecondary program in veterinary technology. Technologists usually need a 4-year bachelor's degree, and technicians need a 2-year associate's degree. Typically, both technologists and technicians must take a credentialing exam and become registered, licensed, or certified, depending on the requirements of the state in which they work. |
| Veterinary Assistants | $36,440 | Veterinary assistants and laboratory animal caretakers handle routine animal care and help scientists, veterinarians, and others with their daily tasks. Most veterinary assistants and laboratory animal caretakers have a high school diploma or equivalent and learn the occupation on the job. |
| The American Board of Veterinary Specialties recognizes 46 distinct veterinary specialties. | | |

Despite the lack of diversity among veterinarians, there are success stories like the story in the Atlanta Journal Constitution, *"Georgia's Critter Fixers: Black vets go from HBCUs to Nat Geo Wild"* profiling how two HBCU students started a veterinary practice and television show. *"It wasn't until my junior year in college that I saw a Black vet,"* he said. That's because fewer than 2 percent of the country's veterinarians look like him.

That vet, Dr. Earnest Corker, inspired Ferguson to continue to follow his heart and become a vet. Corker became not only his mentor, but also mentor to Ferguson's friend and now business partner, Dr. Vernard Hodges.

Ferguson and Hodges graduated from Fort Valley State University and then attended veterinary school at Tuskegee University. The two opened Critter Fixer Veterinary Hospital in 1999, and last year became the newest members of the National Geographic family with their own show, "Critter Fixers: Country Vets."

In addition to the Fort Valley State University Veterinary Science and Public Health program and Tuskegee University College of Veterinary Medicine (which is the oldest HBCU Veterinary School), following are some of the HBCUs with programs in veterinary science:

- The University of Maryland Eastern Shore School of Veterinary Medicine, scheduled to open in the fall of 2026, and unlike Tuskegee University, will be a 3-year program.

- Florida A&M University College of Agriculture and Food Sciences offers a concentration in Pre-Veterinary Medicine to prepare students for veterinary school and a Master of Science in Veterinary Science.

- North Carolina A&T State University College of Agriculture and Environmental Sciences offers a Bachelor Science in Animal Science with a concentration in Pre-Veterinary Medicine to prepare students for veterinary school and a Master of Sciences in Animal Science.

- Delaware State University College of Agriculture offers a Bachelor Science in Animal Science with a concentration in Pre-Veterinary Medicine to prepare students for veterinary school and a Master of Sciences in Animal Science.

There are also HBCUs offering pre-veterinary programs, such as Alabama A&M University, Alabama State University, Alcorn State University, Lincoln University (MO), Prairie View A&M University, and South Carolina State University.

　　　　　　　　　Mychal Wynn

## HBCU Veterinary School Pathways

**Dillard University — Ross University School of Veterinary Medicine:** Students who have completed their undergraduate junior year and have met the academic criteria established through Dillard University and Ross Vet Pathways Program.

**North Carolina A&T State University — Ross University School of Veterinary Medicine:** Students who have completed their undergraduate junior year and have met the academic criteria established through the North Carolina A&T State University and Ross Vet Pathways Program.

**Prairie View A&M University — Ross University School of Veterinary Medicine:** Students who have completed their undergraduate junior year and have met the academic criteria established through the Prairie View A&M University and Ross Vet Pathways Program.

**Tougaloo College — Mississippi State University College of Veterinary Medicine:** Mississippi State School of Veterinary Medicine has an early identification program for Tougaloo students who will be accepted to the program in their junior year based on their academic performance, and will be accepted to the school in their senior year.

**University of Maryland Eastern Shore — Ross University School of Veterinary Medicine:** Students who have completed their undergraduate junior year and have met the academic criteria established through the University of Maryland Eastern Shore and Ross Vet Pathways Program will receive: $1,000 tuition deposit fee waived (as applicable); $100 application fee waived (except where prohibited by law); Priority application consideration; Personal admissions interview.

## Resources

Boards, associations, and veterinarian networking organizations:
- American Animal Hospital Association
- American Association of Equine Veterinary Technicians & Assistants
- American Association of Rehabilitation Veterinarians
- American Association of Veterinary Medical Colleges
- American Association of Veterinary State Boards
- American Association of Wildlife Veterinarians
- American Board of Veterinary Practitioners
- American Board of Veterinary Specialties
- American College of Theriogenologists
- American College of Veterinary Anesthesia and Analgesia
- American College of Veterinary Behaviorists
- American College of Veterinary Ophthalmic Technicians
- American College of Veterinary Ophthalmologists
- American College of Veterinary Pathologists
- American College of Veterinary Pharmacists
- American College of Veterinary Preventive Medicine
- American College of Veterinary Surgeons
- American Society of Veterinary Nephrology and Urology
- American Veterinary Chiropractic Association
- American Veterinary Dental College
- American Veterinary Medical Association
- Association of Shelter Medicine Veterinary Technicians
- Association of Veterinary Anaesthetists
- Association of Veterinary Technician Educators
- Association of Zoo & Exotic Veterinary Nurses
- Association of Zoo Veterinary Technicians
- BlackDVM Network
- Independent Veterinary Cooperative
- National Association of Black Veterinarians
- National Association Veterinary Technicians in America
- Veterinary Nurse Initiative

# In Summary

To fully appreciate the opportunities provided by early acceptance/early assurance or dual degree programs through an HBCU, let's revisit the National Center for Health Workforce Analysis *"State of the U.S. Health Care Workforce, 2023,"* and the underrepresentation of Blacks in virtually all healthcare careers.

| Occupation | Blacks as a Percentage of the Workforce |
|---|---|
| Audiologists | 3.4% |
| Chiropractors | 2.7% |
| Dentists | 4.1% |
| Dental Assistants | 6.8% |
| Dental Hygienists | 3.9% |
| Dietitians and Nutritionists | 12.1% |
| Licensed Practical Nurses | 26.2% |
| Optometrists | 1.9% |
| Opticians | 6.3% |
| Pharmacists | 6.5% |
| Pharmacy Technicians | 13.6% |
| Physicians | 5.0% |
| Physician Assistants | 5.3% |
| Podiatrists | ** |
| Occupational Therapists | 5.2% |
| Physical Therapists | 4.1% |
| Physical Therapist Assistants | 5.6% |
| Radiation Therapists | 6.6% |
| Recreational Therapists | 13.3% |
| Registered Nurses | 11.5% |
| Registered Nurses - Advanced Practice | 7.2% |
| Respiratory Therapists | 13.2% |
| Speech-language Pathologists | 4.9% |
| Veterinarians | 1.5% |
| Veterinarian Assistants | 4.0% |

Pursuing a healthcare pathway into a career where Black students will find themselves underrepresented in every class and in every school setting, must give consideration to the culture of support provided in an HBCU undergraduate program as the student is being prepared to enter into a graduate or medical school setting with a history of discrimination and alienation. While this does not mean that a student will experience either, these are the historical facts.

The competitiveness in applying to graduate school and medical school, and the associated expenses of application fees, exam fees, cost of exam prep, and travel expenses associated with interviewing, can all be avoided through early acceptance/assurance programs. Additionally, when such programs guarantee admission for 1 - 3 students from your school, you are assured of not being the only Black student in the program, and you will be entering a program where your school has developed a reputation for producing highly qualified students.

If all of these reasons were not enough to make this a well-planned and thoughtful strategy, consider the huge cost savings if you can land a scholarship for your undergraduate education with a GPA and test scores that meet the threshold! Even if you cannot land a full scholarship as you enter your undergraduate program, the plethora of scholarship opportunities available through the UNCF and TMCF should allow you to close your financial aid gap and minimize your student loan debt—at least for your undergraduate education.

## Be Deliberate in Your Research

Visit each college's website or perform an internet search on the phrase "college name + guaranteed medical school acceptance" or "hbcu guaranteed medical school assurance pathways" to guide your research into the unique opportunities available through the many partnerships established by HBCUs with other schools, some of which are listed here.

Even HBCUs that do not have early assurance programs are forging partnerships with top medical schools like the Stanford Medical School Racial Equity to Advance Community of Health (REACH) Initiative, which is a set of six programs with a mission of diversifying



Mychal Wynn

healthcare and the biomedical sciences and impacting health inequality nationwide. The REACH-HBMC Summer Program is the nation's only program that collaborates with all four HBMCs, Meharry Medical College, Howard University School of Medicine, Morehouse School of Medicine, and Charles R. Drew University of Medicine and Science. Each summer, a cohort of approximately 50-plus medical students from these schools spend eight weeks as paid research interns in Stanford Medicine labs.

The REACH-HBMC initiative includes:

- **REACH Post-Baccalaureate Research:** This program aims to provide research opportunities and professional development training that enhance each scholar's applications to graduate and medical schools. In addition, we will build a collaborative diverse community that fosters equity and belonging across departments, with the eventual goal of expanding the pipeline of students applying to Stanford graduate and medical schools.

- **REACH Scholars in Health Equity MD/Masters Program:** A five year MD/Masters program that is committed to developing a cohort of physician-leaders with the skills and resources to promote Social Justice and Health Equity. The program will encompass the entirety of the student's medical school education. The program will fully fund tuition and stipend to complete a one year masters program of the student's choice. REACH Scholars in Health Equity programming will provide a foundation in theory; exposure to a wide range of content areas and methodologies; as well as the tools to translate scholarship into advocacy and action. The program will also provide community, mentorship, and networking opportunities.

- **REACH Biosciences PhD Fellowship:** Increases the number of underrepresented and disadvantaged students pursuing research careers in academic medicine by fully funding 2-3 students per year for the first three to four years of their PhD studies. Decouples PhD funding from advisors' grants, giving students the freedom to pursue the areas of study they are most passionate about while giving labs across Stanford Medicine access to a truly diverse pool of outstanding talent to broaden their research perspectives.

The program is also working with 17 undergraduate HBCUs to create opportunities for knowledge exchange and mutual support. Stanford Medicine has hosted leaders from 12 schools for a BioMedicine Think Tank, 16 science faculty members for grant writing workshops, and over the course of two summers nearly 100 students for R Data Science Courses.

**Spelman College Pre-Health Summer Program (PHSP):** A six-week residential experience for recently admitted students interested in pursuing a health professional career. Participants will attend pre-health courses, career development seminars, and peer-tutoring sessions to enhance their critical thinking, oral communication, and analytical skills in preparation for their undergraduate pre-health journey.

## Scholarships

HBCU-specific scholarships are extensively covered in *HBCU Scholarships*. However, to jump start your scholarship research, begin by performing internet searches on phrases containing:

- Race
- Gender
- Field of Study
- Level of Study (i.e., undergraduate, graduate, medical school, etc.)

Following are examples of using these phrases:

- "undergraduate scholarships for black students in stem"
- "graduate fellowships for physical therapists"
- "graduate fellowships for women in stem"
- "graduate fellowships for black students"

Performing an internet search in this way will show pages and pages of scholarships from across the internet. However, to focus your search on UNCF (United Negro College Fund) and TMCF (Thurgood Marshall College Fund) scholarships, use search phrases like the following:

- Example, *"site: uncf.org stem scholarships"* [**site: + uncf.org + stem scholarships**] limits the search to UNCF-affiliated scholarships or scholarships posted on the UNCF website. Continue to change the "stem" part of the phrase to other terms, e.g., women, black male, minority, physical therapy, biomedical engineering, etc.

- Example, *"site: tmcf.org stem scholarships"* [**site: + tmcf.org + stem scholarships**] limits the search to TMCF-affiliated scholarships or scholarships posted on the TMCF website. Continue to change the "stem" part of the phrase to other terms, e.g., women, black male, minority, physical therapy, biomedical engineering, etc.

Begin your search early in your college planning process and expand your search as you learn more about healthcare career pathways. Some of the graduate fellowship programs you should be positioning yourself for as you enter college are:

- Hubert H. Humphrey Fellowship Program

- National Academies Ford Foundation Fellowships

- National Science Foundation Graduate Research Fellowship Program

- Pathwaystoscience.org provides a comprehensive listing of STEM scholarships and fellowships

- College websites like the Rice University Graduate and Postdoctoral Studies and Johns Hopkins University websites can prove to be invaluable resources

Maximize your time by creating a scholarship table or spreadsheet. Add scholarships for which you believe you will qualify for in the future.

# Appendix
# HBCU Listing

## Alabama

Alabama A&M University (TMCF)
Alabama State University (TMCF)
Bishop State Community College (TMCF)
C.A. Fredd Campus of Shelton State Community College (TMCF)
Gadsden State Community College (TMCF)
H Councill Trenholm State Community College (TMCF)
J.F. Drake State Community and Technical College (TMCF)
Lawson State Community College (TMCF)
Miles College (UNCF)
Oakwood University (UNCF)
Shelton State Community College (TMCF)
Stillman College (UNCF)
Talladega College (UNCF)
Tuskegee University (TMCF)/(UNCF)

## Arkansas

Arkansas Baptist College
Philander Smith University (UNCF)
Shorter College
University of Arkansas at Pine Bluff (TMCF)

## California

Charles R. Drew University of Medicine & Science (TMCF)

## Delaware

Delaware State University (TMCF)

## District of Columbia

Howard University (TMCF)/(UNCF)
University of the District of Columbia (TMCF)
University of the District of Columbia-David A Clarke School of Law (TMCF)

## Florida

Bethune-Cookman University (UNCF)
Edward Waters College (UNCF)
Florida Agricultural and Mechanical University (TMCF)
Florida Memorial University (UNCF)

## Georgia

Albany State University (TMCF)
Clark Atlanta University (UNCF)
Fort Valley State University (TMCF)
Interdenominational Theological Center (UNCF)
Morehouse College (UNCF)
Morehouse School of Medicine
Morris Brown College
Paine College (UNCF)
Savannah State University (TMCF)
Spelman College (UNCF)

## Kentucky

Kentucky State University (TMCF)
Simmons College of Kentucky

## Louisiana

Dillard University (UNCF)
Grambling State University (TMCF)
Southern University and A&M College (TMCF)
Southern University at New Orleans (TMCF)
Southern University at Shreveport (TMCF)
Southern University Law Center (TMCF)
Xavier University of Louisiana (UNCF)

## Maryland

Bowie State University (TMCF)
Coppin State University (TMCF)
Morgan State University (TMCF)
University of Maryland Eastern Shore (TMCF)

## Mississippi

Alcorn State University (TMCF)
Coahoma Community College
Jackson State University (TMCF)
Mississippi Valley State University (TMCF)
Rust College (UNCF)
Tougaloo College (UNCF)

## Missouri

Harris-Stowe State University (TMCF)
Lincoln University (MO (TMCF)

## North Carolina

Bennett College (UNCF)
Elizabeth City State University (TMCF)
Fayetteville State University (TMCF)
Johnson C. Smith University (UNCF)
Livingstone College (UNCF)
North Carolina A&T State University (TMCF)
North Carolina Central University (TMCF)
Saint Augustine's University (UNCF)
Shaw University (UNCF)
Winston-Salem State University (TMCF)

## Ohio

Central State University (TMCF)
Wilberforce University (UNCF)

## Oklahoma

Langston University (TMCF)

## Pennsylvania

Cheyney University of Pennsylvania (TMCF)
Lincoln University (PA) (TMCF)

## South Carolina

Allen University (UNCF)
Benedict College (UNCF)
Claflin University (UNCF)
Clinton College

Denmark Technical College (TMCF)
Morris College (UNCF)
South Carolina State University (TMCF)
Voorhees College (UNCF)

## Tennessee

American Baptist College
Fisk University (UNCF)
Lane College (UNCF)
LeMoyne-Owen College (UNCF)
Meharry Medical College
Tennessee State University (TMCF)

## Texas

Huston-Tillotson University (UNCF)
Jarvis Christian College (UNCF)
Paul Quinn College
Prairie View A&M University (TMCF)
Southwestern Christian College
St. Philip's College
Texas College (UNCF)
Texas Southern University (TMCF)
Wiley University (UNCF)

## U.S. Virgin Islands

University of the Virgin Islands (TMCF)

## Virginia

Hampton University
Norfolk State University (TMCF)
Virginia State University (TMCF)
Virginia Union University (UNCF)
Virginia University of Lynchburg

## West Virginia

Bluefield State University (TMCF)
West Virginia State University (TMCF)

                    Mychal Wynn

# References


1890 Land Grant Universities. (2024). Retrieved 9/21/24, from https://www.nifa.usda.gov/sites/default/files/2023-07/NIFA1890LGUs_Map_07-2023.pdf

ABC 11 News Raleigh NC (WTVD). (2024). NCCU students struggle to find housing as university enrolls more freshmen for upcoming school year. Retrieved 9/21/24, from https://www.msn.com/en-us/money/careers/nccu-students-struggle-to-find-housing-as-university-enrolls-more-freshmen-for-upcoming-school-year/ar-BB1pHeHs

ACT Inc. (2024). The Benchmarks. Retrieved 9/21/24, from https://www.act.org/content/act/en/college-and-career-readiness/benchmarks.html

ACT Inc. (2023). Profile Report - National: Graduating Class of 2023. Retrieved 9/21/24, from https://www.act.org/content/dam/act/unsecured/documents/2023-National-ACT-Profile-Report.pdf

ADEA GoDental. (2024). Making Your Application Stand Out. [Video]. YouTube. Retrieved 9/21/24, from https://www.youtube.com/watch?v=QeRNazpNcdU&list=PLCyJCPmOZNT4USaeex9jnuiAcaX8_EDsQ

Albany State University. (2024). Dental Hygiene Program. Retrieved 9/21/24, from https://www.asurams.edu/academic-affairs/dchealthprof/health/dental-hygiene/index.php

All Nursing Schools. (2024). How Can a Paramedic Become an RN? Retrieved 9/21/24, from https://www.allnursingschools.com/registered-nursing/paramedic-to-rn/

American Association of Colleges of Osteopathic Medicine. (2024). About Osteopathic Medicine: Quick Facts. Retrieved 9/21/24, from https://www.aacom.org/become-a-doctor/about-osteopathic-medicine/quick-facts

American Association of Physician Assistants. (2024). What is a PA? Retrieved 9/21/24, from https://www.aapa.org/about/what-is-a-pa/

American Board of Physical Therapy Residency & Fellowship Education. (2020). 2020 Physical Therapist Residency and Fellowship Education Programs Fact Sheet. Retrieved 9/21/24, from https://abptrfe.apta.org/contentassets/7fe7839b307e43cb96eb0002878a463f/2020-residency_fellowship-fact-sheet.pdf

American Dental Association. (2024). The Dentist Workforce – Key Facts. Health Policy Institute. Retrieved 9/21/24, from https://www.ada.org/-/media/project/ada-organization/ada/ada-org/files/resources/research/hpi/hpigraphic_0221_1.

American Dental Education Association. (2024). Deciding where to apply. Retrieved 9/21/24, from https://www.adea.org/GoDental/Application_Prep/The_Admissions_Process/Deciding_where_to_apply.aspx

American Dental Education Association. (2024). Dental Career FAQs. Retrieved 9/21/24, from https://www.adea.org/GoDental/Future_Dentists/FAQ.aspx

American Dental Education Association. (2024). Dental School Interview. Retrieved 9/21/24, from https://www.adea.org/GoDental/Interviews/

American Dental Education Association. (2024). Personal statement. Retrieved 9/21/24, from https://www.adea.org/GoDental/Application_Prep/The_Admissions_Process/Personal_statement.aspx

American Medical Association. (2024). Medical College Admission Test (MCAT). Retrieved 9/21/24, from https://www.ama-assn.org/topics/medical-college-admission-test

American Medical Association. (2024). Reducing disparities in health care | Causes of health disparity | AMA. Retrieved 9/21/24, from https://www.ama-assn.org/delivering-care/health-equity/reducing-disparities-health-care

American Nurses Association. (2024). ANA Nursing Resources Hub: RN-to-MSN. Retrieved 9/21/24, from https://www.nursingworld.org/content-hub/resources/becoming-a-nurse/guide-to-rn-to-msn-programs/

American Optometric Association. (2021). AOA Special Report: Being Black in Optometry.

Retrieved 9/21/24, from https://www.aoa.org/AOA/Documents/About%20the%20AOA/
AOA_Special_Report.pdf

American Physical Therapy Association. (2020). APTA Physical Therapy
Workforce Analysis. Retrieved 9/21/24, from https://www.apta.org/
contentassets/5997bfa5c8504df789fe4f1c01a717eb/apta-workforce-analysis-2020.pdf

American Physical Therapy Association. (2024). Becoming a Physical Therapist Assistant.
Retrieved 9/21/24, from https://www.apta.org/your-career/careers-in-physical-therapy/
becoming-a-pta

American Physical Therapy Association. (2020). Impact of Student Debt on the Physical
Therapy Profession. Retrieved 9/21/24, from https://www.apta.org/contentassets/
ee2d1bb7f9d841c983d0f21bb076bb79/impact-of-student-debt-report.pdf

American Physical Therapy Association. (2024). PT Moves Me Student Recruitment
Campaign. Retrieved 9/21/24, from https://www.apta.org/your-career/careers-in-
physical-therapy/pt-moves-me

American Podiatric Medical Association. (2024). Comparison of Physician Education Between
Doctors of Podiatric Medicine (DPM), Doctors of Medicine (MD), and Doctors of
Osteopathic Medicine (DO). Retrieved 9/21/24, from https://www.apma.org/compare

Anderson, V., & Burdman, P. (2021). A New Calculus for College Admissions: How policy,
practice, and perceptions of high school math education limit equitable access
to college. Just Equations. Retrieved 9/21/24, from https://cdn.prod.website-files.
com/61afa2b5ded66610900a0b97/644aec77a5f4e9c3f54efc28_New-Calc-College-
Admissions-FINAL-update-4-23.pdf (pp. 8-9)

Association of American Medical Colleges. (2023). Medical Student Education: Debt, Costs,
and Loan Repayment Fact Card for the Class of 2023. Retrieved 9/21/24, from https://
store.aamc.org/downloadable/download/sample/sample_id/603/

Association of American Medical Colleges. (2022). Table A-2.1: Undergraduate Institutions
Supplying 15 or More Black or African American (Alone or In Combination) Applicants
to US MD-Granting Medical Schools, 2023-2024. Retrieved 9/21/24, from https://www.
aamc.org/media/5981/download?attachment

Association of American Medical Colleges. (2023). Table A-12: Applicants, First-Time
Applicants, Acceptees, and Matriculants to U.S. MD-Granting Medical Schools by Race/
Ethnicity (Alone) and Gender, 2020-2021 through 2023-2024. Retrieved 9/21/24, from
https://www.aamc.org/media/6046/download?attachment

Association of American Medical Colleges. (2023). Table A-17: MCAT and GPAs for Applicants
and Matriculants to U.S. MD-Granting Medical Schools by Primary Undergraduate
Major, 2023-24. Retrieved 9/21/24, from https://www.aamc.org/media/6061/download

Association of American Medical Colleges. (2024). The Premed Competencies for Entering
Medical Students. Retrieved 9/21/24, from https://students-residents.aamc.org/
real-stories-demonstrating-premed-competencies/premed-competencies-entering-
medical-students

Association of Chiropractic Colleges. (2024). Discover Chiropractic: Best Chiropractic Schools
Guide. Retrieved 9/21/24, from https://discoverchiropractic.org/

Association of Schools and Colleges of Optometry. (2024). OptomCAS Applicant Data Report
- A National Snapshot (2022-23). Retrieved 9/21/24, from https://www.optomcas.org/
wp-content/uploads/2024/02/OptomCAS-Applicant-Data-Report-2022-2023.pdf

BlackDoctors.org. (2024). Retrieved 9/21/24, from https://blackdoctors.org/

Black Doctors USA. (2024). Retrieved 9/21/24, from https://www.blackdoctorsusa.com/

Black EyeCare Perspective. (2024). The 13% Promise. Retrieved 9/21/24, from https://
blackeyecareperspective.com/the-13-promise

Brathwaire, J., Raufman, J., et. al. (2021). What HBCUs Can Teach Us About Culturally
Sustaining Practices. Teachers College at Columbia University. Retrieved 7/28/24, from
https://ccrc.tc.columbia.edu/easyblog/hbcus-culturally-sustaining-practices.html

Brooks, K. (2021). Why the U.S. Needs More Black Physicians. Haverford College. Retrieved

9/21/24, from https://www.haverford.edu/college-communications/news/why-us-needs-more-black-physicians

Brown, L. (2021). Black History Moments in Chiropractic - ACA Today. American Chiropractic Association. Retrieved 9/21/24, from https://www.acatoday.org/news-publications/black-history-moments-in-chiropractic/

Brown University. (2024). Brown-Tougaloo Partnership. Retrieved 9/21/24, from https://tougaloo.brown.edu/

Bureau of Health Workforce. (2024). Health Workforce Research. Retrieved 9/21/24, from https://bhw.hrsa.gov/data-research/review-health-workforce-research

Childs, K. (2022). College of Dentistry Students Serve Patients with Dire Needs Through Remote Area Medical Program. The Dig at Howard University. Retrieved 9/21/24, from https://thedig.howard.edu/all-stories/college-dentistry-students-serve-patients-dire-needs-through-remote-area-medical-program

Churchill, J., & Gudgel, D. (2024). What is an Ophthalmologist vs Optometrist? American Academy of Ophthalmology. Retrieved 9/21/24, from https://www.aao.org/eye-health/tips-prevention/what-is-ophthalmologist

Clanton, N. (2021). Georgia's Critter Fixers: Black vets go from HBCUs to Nat Geo Wild. Atlanta Journal Constitution. Retrieved 9/21/24, from https://www.ajc.com/life/georgias-critter-fixers-black-vets-go-from-hbcus-to-nat-geo-wild-disney/TMD5JICHCFGCDOLHKGPFIZU6ME/

College Factual. (2024). Florida A&M University Demographics & Diversity Report. Retrieved 9/21/24, from https://www.collegefactual.com/colleges/florida-agricultural-and-mechanical-university/student-life/diversity/#location_diversity

College Factual. (2024). Hampton University Demographics & Diversity Report. Retrieved 9/21/24, from https://www.collegefactual.com/colleges/hampton-university/student-life/diversity/#location_diversity

College Factual. (2024). Howard University Demographics & Diversity Report. Retrieved 9/21/24, from https://www.collegefactual.com/colleges/howard-university/student-life/diversity/#location_diversity

College Factual. (2024). Jackson State University Demographics & Diversity Report. Retrieved 9/21/24, from https://www.collegefactual.com/colleges/jackson-state-university/student-life/diversity/#location_diversity

College Factual. (2024). Morehouse College Demographics & Diversity Report. Retrieved 9/21/24, from https://www.collegefactual.com/colleges/morehouse-college/student-life/diversity/#location_diversity

College Factual. (2024). North Carolina A&T State University Demographics & Diversity Report. Retrieved 9/21/24, from https://www.collegefactual.com/colleges/north-carolina-a-and-t-state-university/student-life/diversity/#location_diversity

College Factual. (2024). Southern University and A&M College Demographics & Diversity Report. Retrieved 9/21/24, from https://www.collegefactual.com/colleges/southern-university-and-a-and-m-college/student-life/diversity/#location_diversity

College Factual. (2024). Spelman College Demographics & Diversity Report. Retrieved 9/21/24, from https://www.collegefactual.com/colleges/spelman-college/student-life/diversity/

Commission on Accreditation in Physical Therapy Education. (2021). Aggregate Program Data - 2021 Physical Therapist Education Programs Fact Sheet. Retrieved 9/21/24, from https://www.capteonline.org/globalassets/capte-docs/aggregate-data/archive/pts/2021-2022-aggregate-pt-program-and-salary-data.pdf

Cottman, R., Babbs Jr, R. L., McKinney Edmonds, M., & Hawkins, H. (2022). Being the Change: Black Physical Therapy Leaders in Their Own Words. American Physical Therapy Association. Retrieved 9/21/24, from https://www.apta.org/article/2022/02/16/bhm-being-the-change

Dental Assisting National Board. (2024). Earn Dental Assistant Certification. Retrieved

9/21/24, from https://www.danb.org/certification/earn-dental-assistant-certification

Dingle, L. (2022). HBCU DPT Programs Produce Great PTs: It Shouldn't Be a Secret. American Physical Therapy Association. Retrieved 9/21/24, from https://www.apta.org/article/2022/05/18/hbcu-dpt-programs-produce-great-pts-it-shouldnt-be-a-secret

Dumont, J. A. (2023). 50 Years of Medicine: The Brown-Tougaloo Partnership | The Warren Alpert Medical School of Brown University. Warren Alpert Medical School. Retrieved 9/21/24, from https://medical.brown.edu/news/2023-02-07/brown-tougaloo-eip

Einaudi, P., Gordon, J., & Kang, K. (2022). Baccalaureate Origins of Underrepresented Minority Research Doctorate Recipients. National Center for Science and Engineering Statistics. Retrieved 9/21/24, from Retrieved 9/21/24, from https://stemuscenter.org/

Elliott, A., Alexander, S., Mescher, C., & Deepika, M. (2016). Differences in Physicians' Verbal and Nonverbal Communication With Black and White Patients at the End of Life. Journal of Pain and Symptom Management. Volume 51, Issue 1 p1-8 January 2016

Faubion, D. (2024). Is an ABSN Worth it - (Pros vs Cons). NursingProcess.Org. Retrieved 9/21/24, from https://www.nursingprocess.org/is-absn-worth-it.html

Florida A&M University. (2024). College of Pharmacy & Pharmaceutical Sciences, Institute of Public Health. Retrieved 9/21/24, from https://pharmacy.famu.edu/

Gaines, K. (2024). What Are All the Types of Nurses? Nurse.org. Retrieved 9/21/24, from https://nurse.org/education/types-of-nurses/

Gasman, M., Smith, T., Ye, C., & Nguyen, T.-H. (2017). HBCUs and the Production of Doctors. AIMS Public Health, 4(6), 579-589. 10.3934/publichealth.2017.6.579

Greene, B. (2021). America's First Black Physician Sought to Heal a Nation's Persistent Illness. Smithsonian Magazine. Retrieved 9/21/24, from https://www.smithsonianmag.com/history/james-mccune-smith-america-first-black-physician-180977110/

Hampton University. (2024). Pre Health Partnerships: Hampton University/Virginia-Nebraska Alliance. Retrieved 9/21/24, from https://home.hamptonu.edu/science/pre-health-partnerships/

Hanson, M. (2024). Average Graduate Student Loan Debt. EducationData.org. Retrieved 9/21/24, from https://educationdata.org/average-graduate-student-loan-debt

Harvard University. (2024). How Aid Works. Retrieved 9/21/24, from https://college.harvard.edu/financial-aid/how-aid-works

Harvard University. (2024). Tuition and Fees. Retrieved 9/21/24, from https://registrar.fas.harvard.edu/tuition-and-fees

HBCUBuzz. (2011). Dillard University Partners with Texas Chiropractic College. Retrieved 9/21/24, from https://hbcubuzz.com/2011/08/dillard-university-partners-with-texas-chiropractic-college/

HBCU Colleges. (2024). HBCU Nursing Schools - 2024 Ranking. Retrieved 9/21/24, from https://hbcu-colleges.com/nursing

HBCU Connect. (2024). Top 50 Employers of HBCU Students & Graduates. Retrieved 9/21/24, from https://hbcuconnect.com/top50employers.shtml

Hillman, N. (2023). Geography of Opportunity Series | Brief #1 - How Many Students Go Out-of-State for College? The Institute for College Access & Success. Retrieved 9/21/24, from https://ticas.org/wp-content/uploads/2023/11/Hillman-Geography-of-Opportunity-Brief-1_2023.pdf

Hoffman, K., Trawalter, S., Axt, J., & Oliver, M. N. (2016). Racial bias in pain assessment and treatment recommendations, and false beliefs about biological differences between blacks and whites. Proceedings of the National Academy of Sciences, 113 (13), 4296-4301.

Howard University. (2024). College of Dentistry: Doctor of Dental Surgery | Dentistry. Retrieved 9/21/24, from https://dentistry.howard.edu/education/programs-and-admissions/predoctoral-programs/doctor-dental-surgery

HOSA. (2024). HOSA-Future Health Professionals. Retrieved 9/21/24, from https://hosa.org/wp-content/uploads/2022/11/HOSA-NatFactSheet-2023-v7-WEB.pdf

Howard University. (2024). College of Pharmacy. Retrieved 9/21/24, from https://pharmacy.howard.edu/

Hrabowski, F. A., & Henderson, P. H. (2021). Reimagining Science and Engineering at the Frontier. Issues in Science and Technology. Issues in Science and Technology. Retrieved 9/21/24, from https://issues.org/nothing-succeeds-like-success-underrepresented-minorities-stem/

Incredible Health. (2024). 2024 Compact Nursing States. Retrieved 9/21/24, from https://www.incrediblehealth.com/nursing-compact-states/

Indeed. (2024). 14 Careers in Optometry (Plus Salaries, Duties and FAQ). Retrieved 9/21/24, from https://www.indeed.com/career-advice/finding-a-job/careers-in-optometry

Indeed. (2024). 16 Pharmacy-Related Career Options To Consider (With Salary). Retrieved 9/21/24, from https://www.indeed.com/career-advice/finding-a-job/pharmacy-career-options

Indeed. (2024). Doctor of Chiropractic: 12 Career Options for Degree-Holders. Retrieved 9/21/24, from https://www.indeed.com/career-advice/finding-a-job/jobs-for-chiropractic-degree

International Medical Aid. (2022). Dental School Acceptance Rates: The Definitive Guide (updated 2024). Retrieved 9/21/24, from https://medicalaid.org/dental-school-acceptance-rates-comprehensive-list-of-all-us-dental-schools-average-gpa-average-dat-scores-acceptance-rates/

Jividen, S. (2023). Top 10 Best HBCU Nursing Programs for 2024. Nurse.org. Retrieved 9/21/24, from https://nurse.org/education/hbcu-nursing-programs/

Johns Hopkins. (2024). Chiropractic Medicine: What is chiropractic medicine? Retrieved 9/21/24, from https://www.hopkinsmedicine.org/health/wellness-and-prevention/chiropractic-medicine

Journal of Blacks in Higher Education. (2019). A New Pathway for Grambling State University Students to Earn Chiropractic Doctorates. Retrieved 9/21/24, from https://jbhe.com/2019/04/a-new-pathway-for-grambling-state-university-students-to-earn-chiropractic-doctorates/

Ko, N. (2023). The Best HBCU Nursing Programs. NurseJournal. Retrieved 9/21/24, from https://nursejournal.org/degrees/hbcu-nursing-programs/

Kowarski, I., & Wood S. (2023). 15 Medical Schools With the Highest Proportion of Black Students. U.S. News & World Reports. Retrieved 9/21/24, from https://www.usnews.com/education/best-graduate-schools/top-medical-schools/slideshows/medical-schools-with-the-most-african-american-students

LaPonsie, M. (2022). 10 Best Health Care Jobs That Don't Require Medical School. US News Money. Retrieved 9/21/24, from https://money.usnews.com/careers/articles/the-best-medical-jobs-that-dont-require-medical-school

Lane, R. (2021). Average Nursing Student Debt: How Much Do Nurses Owe? NerdWallet. Retrieved 9/21/24, from https://www.nerdwallet.com/article/loans/student-loans/average-nursing-student-debt

Lloyd, S. (2006). Howard University College of Medicine History. Retrieved 10/14/24, from https://medicine.howard.edu/about/history

Louis, D., Phillips, L., Louis, S., & Smith, A. (2024). Historically Black Colleges And Universities: Undergraduate Research, Mentoring And The Graduate Pipeline. Prospectives on Undergraduate Research and Mentoring, 4(1), 1-4. Retrieved 9/21/24, from https://eloncdn.blob.core.windows.net/eu3/sites/923/2019/06/Louis-et-al-PURM-4.1-1.pdf

Luthi, B. (2024). What Is The Average Pharmacy School Debt? Bankrate.com. Retrieved 9/21/24, from https://www.bankrate.com/loans/student-loans/average-pharmacy-school-debt/

Ly, D. P., Seabury, S. A., & Jena, A. B. (2016). Differences in incomes of physicians in the United States by race and sex: observational study. BMJ 2016; 353:i2923 doi:10.1136/bmj.i2923

Mattson, K. (2020). Veterinary educational debt continues to rise. American Veterinary

Medical Association. Retrieved 9/21/24, from https://www.avma.org/javma-news/2020-12-15/veterinary-educational-debt-continues-rise

Meharry Medical College. (2024). About the School of Dentistry. Retrieved 9/21/24, from https://home.mmc.edu/school-of-dentistry/about-the-school-of-dentistry/

Meharry Medical College. (2024). School of Dentistry Patient Care. Retrieved 9/21/24, from https://home.mmc.edu/school-of-dentistry/dental-care/

Mertz, E., Calvo, J., Wides, C., & Gates, P. (2017). The Black dentist workforce in the United States. Journal of public health dentistry. 77(2), 136–147.

Mescher, C., Mohan, D., Barnato, A., Elliott, A., & Alexander, S. (2015). Differences in Physicians' Verbal and Nonverbal Communication With Black and White Patients at the End of Life. Journal of Pain and Symptom Management.

Morehouse School of Medicine. (2018). Celebrating Her Service: Dr. Truddie Darden Retires After Nearly 30 Years. Morehouse School of Medicine. Retrieved 9/21/24, from https://www.msm.edu/blog/2018/celebrating-her-service-dr-truddie-darden-retires-after-nearly-30-years.php

Moultry, A.M. (2021). The Evolving Role of Historically Black Pharmacy Schools in a Changing Environment. American Journal of Pharmaceutical Education Volume 85, Issue 9, 8589, October 01, 2021.

Murphy, B. (2024). DO vs. MD: How much does the medical school degree type matter? American Medical Association. Retrieved 9/21/24, from https://www.ama-assn.org/medical-students/preparing-medical-school/do-vs-md-how-much-does-medical-school-degree-type-matter

Murphy, B. (2021). Which undergrad majors are best for med school? American Medical Association. Retrieved 9/21/24, from https://www.ama-assn.org/medical-students/preparing-medical-school/which-undergrad-majors-are-best-med-school

National Board of Chiropractic Examiners. (2024). Chiropractic Education. Retrieved 9/21/24, from https://www.nbce.org/about-nbce/chiropractic-care/chiropractic-education/

National Center for Education Statistics. (2024). Advanced mathematics and science courses (97). Retrieved 9/21/24, from https://nces.ed.gov/fastfacts/display.asp?id=97

National Center for Education Statistics. (2024). Beginning College Students Who Change Their Majors Within 3 Years of Enrollment. Retrieved 9/21/24, from https://nces.ed.gov/pubs2018/2018434/index.asp

National Center for Education Statistics. (2016). Indicator 13: High School Coursetaking (Last Updated: August 2016). Retrieved 9/21/24, from https://nces.ed.gov/programs/raceindicators/indicator_rcd.asp

National Center for Health Workforce Analysis. (2024). State of the U.S. Health Care Workforce, 2023. Bureau of Health Workforce. Retrieved 9/21/24, from https://bhw.hrsa.gov/sites/default/files/bureau-health-workforce/data-research/state-of-the-health-workforce-report-2023.pdf

National Library of Medicine. (2024). National Center for Biotechnology Information: 2021 National Healthcare Quality and Disparities Report. Retrieved 9/21/24, from https://www.ncbi.nlm.nih.gov/books/NBK578535/figure/ch2.fig18/

National Science Foundation. (2024). HBCU STEM Undergraduate Success Research Center. Retrieved 9/21/24, from https://stemuscenter.org/

NaturalHealers. (2024). Chiropractor Schooling Requirements (Degrees & How Long They Take). Retrieved 9/21/24, from https://www.naturalhealers.com/chiropractic/degree/

Northeast College of Health Sciences. (2024). What Undergrad Degrees Prepare You for Chiropractic School? Retrieved 9/21/24, from https://www.northeastcollege.edu/learn/what-undergrad-degrees-prepare-you-for-chiropractic-school

Odom Walker, K., Moreno, G., & Grumbach, K. (2012). The association among specialty, race, ethnicity, and practice location among California physicians in diverse specialties. Junior National Medical Association, 104(1-2), 46-52. 10.1016/s0027-9684(15)30126-7

Oppenheimer, T. H. (2024). How to Become an Optician. Nurse.org. Retrieved 9/21/24, from https://nurse.org/healthcare/optician/

Porter, T. (2023). Is Dental School Worth The Student Debt? Bankrate.com. Retrieved 9/21/24, from https://www.bankrate.com/loans/student-loans/average-dental-school-debt/

Registered Nursing.org. (2024). RN to BSN Requirements: A Complete Guide. Retrieved 9/21/24, from https://www.registerednursing.org/rn-to-bsn/requirements/

Rivera, H. (2024). Average Medical School Debt For 2023-24. Bankrate.com. Retrieved 9/21/24, from https://www.bankrate.com/loans/student-loans/average-medical-school-debt/

Roberts, A. (2024). LPN to BSN. Nursing Education. Retrieved 9/21/24, from https://nursingeducation.org/degrees/lpn-to-bsn/

Salary.com. (2024). Podiatrist Salary in the United States. Retrieved 9/21/24, from https://www.salary.com/research/salary/alternate/podiatrist-salary

Sax, K. (2024). Historically Black Colleges and Universities Nursing Programs. Registered Nursing. Retrieved 9/21/24, from https://www.registerednursing.org/hbcu-nursing-schools/

Solano, K. (2019). HPI publishes findings into racial disparities in oral health. American Dental Association. Retrieved 9/21/24, from https://adanews.ada.org/ada-news/2021/april/hpi-publishes-findings-into-racial-disparities-in-oral-health

Tennessee State University. (2024). AAS in Dental Hygiene Program. Retrieved 9/21/24, from https://www.tnstate.edu/dentalhygiene/

Tiako, M., Wages, J., & Perry, S. (2022). Black Medical Students' Sense of Belonging and Confidence in Scholastic Abilities at Historically Black vs Predominantly White Medical Schools: a Prospective Study. J Gen Intern Med, 1(38), 122-124.

U.S. Bureau of Labor Statistics. (2024). Occupational Outlook Handbook: Chiropractors. Retrieved 9/21/24, from https://www.bls.gov/ooh/healthcare/chiropractors.htm

U.S. Bureau of Labor Statistics. (2024). Occupational Outlook Handbook: Dentists. Retrieved 9/21/24, from https://www.bls.gov/ooh/healthcare/dentists.htm#tab-8

U.S. Bureau of Labor Statistics. (2024). Occupational Outlook Handbook: Healthcare Occupations. Retrieved 9/21/24, from https://www.bls.gov/ooh/healthcare/

U.S. Bureau of Labor Statistics. (2024). Occupational Outlook Handbook: Optometrists Occupations. Retrieved 9/21/24, from https://www.bls.gov/ooh/healthcare/optometrists.htm

U.S. Bureau of Labor Statistics. (2024). Occupational Outlook Handbook: Pharmacy Occupations. Retrieved 9/21/24, from https://www.bls.gov/ooh/healthcare/pharmacists.htm

U.S. Bureau of Labor Statistics. (2024). Occupational Outlook Handbook: Physical Therapists Occupations. Retrieved 9/21/24, from https://www.bls.gov/ooh/healthcare/physical-therapists.htm

U.S. Bureau of Labor Statistics. (2024). Occupational Outlook Handbook: Physician and Surgeons. Retrieved 9/21/24, from https://www.bls.gov/ooh/healthcare/physicians-and-surgeons.htm#tab-1

U.S. Bureau of Labor Statistics. (2024). Occupational Outlook Handbook: Veterinarians. Retrieved 9/21/24, from https://www.bls.gov/ooh/healthcare/veterinarians.htm

U.S. Department of Education. (2024). College Scorecard. Compare | College Scorecard — Spelman College and Morgan State University. Retrieved 9/21/24, from https://collegescorecard.ed.gov/compare/?toggle%3Dinstitutions%26s%3D141060%26s%3D163453

U.S. Department of Education. (2024). College Scorecard. Compare | College Scorecard — Tuskegee University and Alabama State University. Retrieved 9/21/24, from https://collegescorecard.ed.gov/compare/?toggle%3Dinstitutions%26s%3D102377%26s%3D100724

U.S. News.com. (2024). 2024 Best Medical Schools: Research. Retrieved 9/21/24, from https://www.usnews.com/best-graduate-schools/top-medical-schools

United Negro College Fund. (2016). Fewer Resources, More Debt: Loan Debt Burdens Students at Historically Black Colleges and Universities. Retrieved 9/21/24, from https://uncf.org/wp-content/uploads/reports/FINAL_HBCU_Loan_Debt_Burden_Report.pdf?_ga=2.262428428.143846847.1522074542-2044485191.1493842567

University of California. (2024). Statement on Mathematics - BOARS Area C Workgroup Stage 1 Report. Retrieved 9/21/24, from https://senate.universityofcalifornia.edu/_files/committees/boars/documents/boarsacwphase1report-20240221.pdf

University of Maryland - Baltimore County. (2024). Meyerhoff Scholars Program. Retrieved 9/21/24, from https://meyerhoff.umbc.edu/

University of Maryland Eastern Shore. (2024). The School of Pharmacy and Health Professions. Retrieved 9/21/24, from https://wwwcp.umes.edu/shp/

University of Southern California. (2024). Tuition and Financial Aid. Retrieved 9/21/24, from https://dpt.usc.edu/hybrid-dpt-program/admissions/tuition-and-financial-aid/

University of St. Augustine for Health Sciences. (2024). 5 Best Undergraduate Degrees for Physical Therapy. Retrieved 9/21/24, from https://www.usa.edu/blog/5-best-undergraduate-degrees-for-physical-therapy/

USDA 1890 National Scholars Program. (2024). U.S. Department of Agriculture. Retrieved, 9/21/24, from https://www.usda.gov/partnerships/1890NationalScholars

Williams, D., & Mullan, F. (2017). Why we need more black doctors. STAT News. Retrieved 9/21/24, from https://www.statnews.com/2017/01/16/black-doctors-shortage-education/

Winston-Salem State University. (2024). Accelerated BSN. Retrieved 9/21/24, from https://www.wssu.edu/admissions/programs/accelerated-bsn.html

Winston-Salem State University. (2024). BSN Holistic Admission Nursing. Retrieved 9/21/24, from https://www.wssu.edu/academics/colleges-and-departments/school-of-health-sciences/division-of-nursing/holistic-admission-nursing.html

Winston-Salem State University. (2024). Nursing Major, BSN Catalog. Retrieved 9/21/24, from https://catalog.wssu.edu/preview_program.php?catoid=40&poid=2914&returnto=3989

Wondwossen, W. (2020). The science behind HBCU success | NSF. National Science Foundation. Retrieved 9/21/24, from https://new.nsf.gov/science-matters/science-behind-hbcu-success

Xavier University. (2024). Xavier University: Direct Entry MSN Programs: A Comprehensive Guide. Retrieved 9/21/24, from https://online.xavier.edu/direct-entry-msn-programs-a-comprehensive-guide/

Xavier University of Louisiana. (2024). 2023-2024 General Tuition Cost & Fees. Retrieved 9/21/24, from https://www.xula.edu/financialaid/general-tuition-cost-fees.html

Xavier University of Louisiana. (2024). Academic Scholarships: Board of Trustees Scholarship. Retrieved 9/21/24, from https://www.xula.edu/financialaid/academic-scholarships/

Xavier University of Louisiana. (2024). College of Pharmacy - COP Pre-Pharmacy Requirements. Retrieved 9/21/24, from https://www.xula.edu/assets/prepharmacy-requirements-form-8.18.20211.pdf

Xavier University of Louisiana. (2024). Special Programs for Premeds. Retrieved 9/21/24, from https://www.xula.edu/premed/special-programs-for-premeds.html

Zippia. (2004). Podiatrist Demographics and Statistics. Retrieved 9/21/24, from https://www.zippia.com/podiatrist-jobs/demographics/

# Tables


Median wages for healthcare occupations, vii
Percentage of Black employment by healthcare occupations, viii
Chiropractic career and salary data, 23
Percentage of Black employment in chiropractor workforce, 24
Dental career and salary data, 29-30
Percentage of Black employment in oral health workforce, 24
Physician career and salary data, 40
Percentage of Black employment in physician workforce, 40
Colleges/Universities with largest number of Black students accepted into medical school, 41
Medical school acceptance rates, 45
Nursing career and salary data, 56-59
Percentage of Black RN, LPN, and APRN employment in the nursing workforce, 59
Optometry career and salary data, 71-74
Black-owned Eyewear Brands, 82
Pharmacy career and salary data, 83-84
Percentage of Black employment in pharmacist workforce, 85
Physical therapy career and salary data, 92-93
Percentage of Black employment in physical therapist workforce, 94
Percentage of Blacks receiving physical therapist residencies and fellowships
Percentage of Black faculty in physical therapy programs
Podiatry career and salary data, 103
Veterinary career and salary data, 106-107
Black underrepresentation across healthcare occupations, 111

# Index


**Symbols**

12 ADA-Recognized Dental Specialties  29

15 Medical Schools With the Highest Proportion of Black Students  45

50 Years of Medicine: The Brown-Tougaloo Partnership  xiii

1890 land-grant universities  108

1890 National Scholars Program  108

2021 National healthcare Quality and Disparities Report  88

(NROTC) – Nurse Option  69

**A**

A New Calculus for College Admissions: How Policy, Practice, and Perceptions of High School Math Education Limit Equitable Access to College  4

ABC 11 News Raleigh NC (WTVD)  xviii

Accelerated Scholars Program  51

ACT college-readiness benchmarks  5

ACT Profile Report  5

ADHA Institute for Oral Health  36

Advanced mathematics and science courses  3

Aetna Health Professions Partnership Initiative 35

Aisha Morris Moultry  86

Alabama A&M University  47, 53, 89, 118

Alabama State University  xix, 47, 50, 53, 98, 118

Albany State University  33, 34, 50, 64, 100, 119

Alcorn State University  50, 64, 65, 121

allnurses.com  62

Alpert Medical School  46, 126

American Academy of Ophthalmology  76, 79, 83

American Association of Colleges of Osteopathic Medicine  42

American Association of Medical Colleges  8, 10, 15, 22

American Association of Physician Assistants  42

American Black Chiropractic Association  26, 28

American Board of Ophthalmology  80, 83

American Board of Physical Therapy Residency & Fellowship Education  95, 104

American Dental Association  30, 33, 36, 39

American Dental Education Association  32, 39

American Medical Association  14, 42, 54

American Optometric Association  75, 85

American Optometric Student Association  75

American Physical Therapy Association  95, 98, 99, 100, 104

American University of Antigua  48

APTA Physical Therapy Workforce Analysis  95

Associate Degree in Nursing  xvi, 60

Association of American Medical Colleges  xvi, 14, 41, 54

Association of Chiropractic Colleges  25

Association of Schools and Colleges of Optometry  78-79

Atlanta Journal Constitution  109

Atlanta University Center  xviii

Auburn University Harrison College of Pharmacy  91

Auburn University School of Kinesiology  102

Augusta University  66

Average ACT Math scores, by racial group  5

Average ACT Science scores, by racial group  6

Average Graduate Student Loan Debt  xvi

Average Nursing Student Debt: How Much Debt Do Nurses Have?  xvi

average student loan debt for dentists  xv

average student loan debt for pharmacists  xv

average student loan debt for physical therapists  xv

average student loan debt for veterinarians  xv

**B**

Bachelor of Science in Nursing  xvi, 60, 61, 62, 63, 64, 66

backwards mapping  xv

Baylor  13, 21, 45, 53

Baylor College of Medicine  45, 53

Beginning College Students Who Change Their Majors Within 3 Years of Enrollment  12

Being Black in Optometry  75

Benedict College  xviii, 15

Bennett College  89

Bethune- Cookman University  50

BigFuture  xix

Black Academicians in Physical Therapy  96

BlackDoctors.org  xi, 55, 108

Black Doctors USA  xi, 108

Black Medical Students' Sense of Belonging and Confidence in Scholastic Abilities at Historically Black vs Predominantly White Medical Schools 7
Black-owned Eyewear Brands 82
Blacks as a Percentage of the Workforce 111
Board of Trustees Scholarship 13
Boston University 21, 45, 46, 50
Boston University Chobanian & Avedisian School of Medicine 46
Boston University School of Medicine 45
Boston University School of Public Health 50
Bowie State University 65, 79, 120
Brendan Murphy 14, 42
Bristol Myers Squibb 9
Broward County High School 75
Brown University xiii, xiv, 45, 46, 52
Brown University Medical School 45, 52
Burroughs Wellcome Scholars 47, 52
BUSPH 50

**C**
California Community Colleges Guaranteed HBCU Transfer Pathways v
CAM Program 51
Cardinal Health 9
Carson, California x
Case Western Reserve 21
Central Tennessee College 31
Certified Nursing Assistant (CNA 59
Charles R Drew University of Medicine and Science 20
Cheyney University 89
Chiropractor Workforce 24
Claflin University xviii, 15, 65
Clark Atlanta University xix, 119
Cleveland State University 96
Coahoma Community College 65
Coalition of Black Physical Therapists Facebook Group 97
CollegeBoard xix
College Factual xix, 8
College Navigator xix
College Scorecard xix
Columbia University 1, 45
Commission on Accreditation in Physical Therapy Education 96
Compact Nursing States 63
Coppin State University 65
Cornell University 8
Council for Higher Education Accreditation 62, 70
Council on Chiropractic Education 26, 28
Critter Fixers: Country Vets 109

Cultural competence ix
cultural incompetence x
culturally sustaining practices 1
**D**
Dartmouth 13, 53
Dartmouth Geisel School of Medicine 53
Delaware State University 64, 65, 110, 119
Delaware State University College of Agriculture 110
Dental Assisting National Board 33, 39
Dental Corps 37
Dental School Acceptance Rates: The Definitive Guide (2024) 32
Differences in incomes of physicians in the United States by race and sex: observational study x, 127
Dillard University 27, 46, 50, 65, 69, 111, 119
Division of Biokinesiology and Physical Therapy at the University of Southern California 102
DO vs. MD: How much does the medical school degree type matter? 42
Dr. Devin Sasser 75
Dr. Earnest Corker 109
Dr. Fred Rubel 24
Dr. James Carter ix
Dr. Jason Compton 75
Dr. Karen McCord v
Dr. Kevin Mason x
Dr. Sherrol Reynolds 75
Dr. Tonya Fancher 15
Dr. Truddie Darden x
Dr. Vernard Hodges 109
Dual degree programs xiii
Duke University 45
**E**
Early Identification Program xiii, 46, 48, 52
East Carolina Brody School of Medicine 45, 49
Eastern Virginia Medical School 48
Edward Via College of Osteopathic Medicine 50, 52
Edward Waters University 66
Emory University 45, 67
Emory University Nell Hodgson Woodruff School of Nursing 67
Erie College of Osteopathic Medicine School of Dental Medicine 36
Erin N vi, xii, xiv
**F**
Fayetteville State University 64, 65, 89, 121
Fewer Resources More Debt: Loan Debt Burdens Students at Historically Black

     Mychal Wynn

Colleges & Universities xvi
financial literacy 20
findmyhbcu.com xix
first Black Doctor of Chiropractic 24
Fisk University 34, 49, 66, 79
Florida A&M College of Pharmacy & Pharmaceutical Sciences, Institute of Public Health 87
Florida A&M University xviii, 8, 9, 41, 50, 64, 65, 79, 87, 88, 98, 109
Florida A&M University College of Agriculture and Food Sciences 109
Florida Memorial University 50, 119
Fort Valley State University 89, 109, 119
Fort Valley State University Veterinary Science and Public Health 109
Frederick Douglass xx
Future Scholars Summer Research Bridge Program 102

**G**

Galen College of Nursing 66
Gates Millennium Scholar xviii
Georgetown University 51
George Washington School of Medicine 47
Georgia's Critter Fixers: Black vets go from HBCUs to Nat Geo Wild 109
Grambling State University 27, 64, 119

**H**

Hackensack Meridian Health 9
Hampton University xviii, xix, 8, 11, 34, 41, 43, 46, 47, 48, 50, 64, 65, 81, 82, 88, 98, 106
Hampton University School of Pharmacy 88
Hampton University/Virginia-Nebraska Alliance 11
Harvard University 8, 9, 13
Haverford College ix
HBCU and the Production of Doctors 9
HBCU DPT Programs Produce Great PTs: It Shouldn't Be a Secret 99
HBCU STEM Undergraduate Success Research Center 2, 7
HBCUBuzz 27
hbcuconnect.com 62
Healthcare Occupations vii, 56
Health Disparities Clinical Summer Research Fellowship Program 35
Health Professional Scholarship Program 38
Health Services Collegiate Program 38
Henry Schein 38
HOSA-Future Health Professionals 18, 126
Howard University xi, xviii, 8, 9, 15, 20, 27, 32, 41, 43, 45, 49, 64, 66, 69, 79, 87, 88, 89,
97, 99, 115, 119
Howard University College of Arts and Sciences' Human Performance 27
Howard University College of Dentistry 15, 32
Howard University College of Medicine xi, 20, 127
Howard University College of Nursing 43, 64, 66
Howard University College of Nursing and Allied Health Sciences 43, 64, 66
Howard University College Pharmacy 87
Howard University Department of Physician Assistant 43
Howard University Doctor of Dental Surgery 32
How Many Students Go Out-of-State for College? 8
HPI publishes findings into racial disparities in oral health 36
Hrabowski 9
Hubert H. Humphrey Fellowship Program 117

**I**

Illinois College of Optometry 82
Institute for College Access & Success 8
Institute of Medicine ix
International Medical Aid 32
It wasn't until my junior year in college that I saw a Black vet 109
Ivy League xii, 13, 41

**J**

Jackson State University 8, 41
James McCune Smith xx
Jim Crow train 96
Johns Hopkins University 24, 41, 118
Johnson C. Smith University 90

**K**

Kaiser Permanente Bernard J. Tyson School of Medicine 22
Kamala Harris xiv
Kennesaw Mountain High School Academy of Mathematics, Science, and Technology Magnet Program xii
Kentucky State University 49, 65, 119
Kimber Solano 36

**L**

LaDonna Dingle 99
Lake Erie College of Osteopathic Medicine School of Dentistry 35
Langston University 99, 121
LECOM 35, 52, 91, 106
Lincoln Memorial University DeBusk College

of Osteopathic Medicine  48
Lincoln University (MO)  64, 110
Logan University College of Chiropractic
    26-27
LSU Dental School  36

**M**
Macon & Joan Brock Virginia Health Sciences
    at Old Dominion University  48
Marshall University School of Medicine  48
Marshall University School of Medicine
    Summer Academy Program  48
Maryalene LaPonsie  11
Mary McKinney Edmonds  96
Maximus  9
Mayo Clinic  21, 45, 53
Mayo Clinic School of Medicine  45, 53
MCAT  xiii, 4, 42, 46, 47, 49, 50, 51, 52, 54
Medical College Admission Test  42
Medical Corps  37
Medical Student Education: Debt, Costs, and
    Loan Repayment Fact Card for the Class
    of 2023  xvi
Meharry Medical College  15, 20, 31, 32, 34,
    44, 45, 48, 49, 115
Meharry Medical College Physician Assistant
    Sciences  44
Meharry Medical College School of Dentistry
    15, 31-32, 34
merit-based scholarships  13
Meyerhoff Scholars Program  9
Michigan State  13, 45, 53
Michigan State University SMART Initiative
    53
Miles College  79, 118
Military Treatment Facilities  22
Mississippi State University College of
    Veterinary Medicine  112
Morehouse College  x, xviii, xix, 7, 8, 41, 46,
    49, 119
Morehouse School of Medicine 20, 43
Morgan State University  xix, 20, 35, 41, 46, 65
Mychal-David Wynn  iv, v

**N**
National Association of Black Physical
    Therapists  96, 104
National Board of Chiropractic Examiners
    25, 28
National Center for Education Statistics  xix,
    3, 12
National Center for Health Workforce Analysis
    vii, 24, 30, 40, 59, 86, 114
National Council Licensure Examination  63,
    72

National Geographic  109
National Library of Medicine  88
National Optometric Association Mentorship
    Program  79
National School of Chiropractic  24
National Science Foundation  2, 6, 7, 117
National Science Foundation Graduate
    Research Fellowship Program  117
NaturalHealers  24
Naval Reserve Officers Training Corps  69
Navy Dental Corps  37
Navy Medicine (NM) Internship Program  37
Navy Nurse Candidate Program  69
Navy Nurse Corps  69, 70
NCLEX  63, 72
need-based financial aid policy  13
Nerdwallet  xvi
Nick Hillman  8
Norfolk State University  65
North Carolina A&T State University  xviii, 4, 8,
    9, 34, 35, 41, 45, 47, 50, 65, 109, 111, 112
North Carolina A&T State University College
    of Agriculture and Environmental
    Sciences  109
North Carolina Central University  xviii, 35, 46,
    50, 82, 90
Northeast College of Health Sciences  25
Nova Southeastern University College of
    Optometry  82
Nova Southern University College of
    Optometry  75
Nurse Corps  37, 69, 70
NursingJournal.org  61
nursingprocess.org  62, 126
NYU Grossman School of Medicine  22

**O**
Oakwood University  41, 47, 49, 50, 53, 64,
    118
OAT  81
Ochsner Health  44
Ohio State University  45
oldest HBCU medical school  xi
oldest HBCU Veterinary School  109
Optometry Admissions Test  81

**P**
Pathwaystoscience.org  117
Penn  13, 21, 48, 49
Penn PASS  49
Penn State University College of Medicine  48
Pennsylvania College of Optometry at Salus
    University  80
Pennsylvania State University College of
    Medicine  43

Pfizer 9
Pharmacist Workforce 85
Physical Therapist Centralized Application Service 101
Physicians and Surgeons 40
Physician Workforce 40
Poston Foundation 78
Prairie View A&M University 41, 50, 64, 65, 80
Premed Competencies for Entering Medical Students 15
Princeton University 41
Professional Competencies 16
PTCAS 101
PTMovesMe Campaign 98

**R**
REACH 115, 116
REACH-HBMC Summer Program 115
Rice University Graduate and Postdoctoral Studies 118
RNCareers.org 63
Rocovich Scholars Program 50
Ross University School of Medicine 49, 52
Ross University School of Veterinary Medicine 111, 112
Ross Vet Pathways Program 111, 112
Roswell, Georgia x
RUSCH 19
Rush University College of Nursing 67
Rutgers School of Dental Medicine 35
Ryan Lane xvi

**S**
Saint Katharine Drexel 89
Salary.com 105
Salus University Pennsylvania College of Optometry 80
Savannah State University 79, 119
Science Competencies 18
Select Scholars Program 50
Sisters of the Blessed Sacrament 89
S.M.I.L.E. 38
South Carolina State University 110
Southern University and A&M College 8, 64, 65, 69, 119
Southern University of Shreveport Louisiana 34
Spelman College xix, 5, 7, 8, 9, 19, 35, 41, 47, 49, 50, 51, 52, 66, 67, 79, 82, 99, 102, 116, 119
Spelman College Pre-Health Summer Program 116
Stanford Medical School Racial Equity to Advance Community of Health 115
Stanford University 8

State Board of Dentistry 33
State of the U.S. Health Care Workforce, 2023 vii, 24, 30, 40, 59, 86, 114
State University of New York College of Optometry 75
State University of New York Upstate College of Medicine 51
STAT News ix
Stillman College 47, 53, 118
Student Mentoring with Immersive Learning and Enrichment 38
SUNY Downstate Medical School 54
SUNY Upstate Medical University College of Medicine 47
SURF 19
Syracuse University 41

**T**
TCU Anne Burnett Marion School of Medicine 48
Teachers College at Columbia University 1, 124
Temple University 45
Tennessee State University xviii, 33, 34, 50, 79, 99
Texas Chiropractic College 26-27
Texas Southern University College of Pharmacy & Health Sciences 88
The Aetna Health Professions Partnership Initiative 35
The association among specialty, race, ethnicity, and practice location among California physicians in diverse specialties x
The Best HealthCare Jobs That Don't Require Medical School 11
The Black Dentist Workforce 36
The Dentists Workforce - Key Facts 30
The Evolving Role of Historically Black Pharmacy Schools in a Changing Environment 86
The Hundred-Seven xix
The Perelman School of Medicine 21
The science behind HBCU success 6, 7
The Uniformed Services University F. Edward Hébert School of Medicine 21
Thinking and Reasoning Competencies 18
Thurgood Marshall College Fund 13, 15, 117
TMCF 13, 15, 114, 117, 118, 119
top 8 producers of Black students who earn PhDs 8
Tougaloo College xiii, 46, 47, 52, 67, 90, 112
Training in Urban Medicine and Public Health 19

TRIUMPH 19
Tulane 13, 45, 54, 69
Tulane University Medical School 45, 54
Tuskegee University xviii, xix, 4, 15, 35, 36,
    41, 47, 50, 52, 53, 90, 91, 106, 109, 118

**U**

UAB School of Dentistry 36
UC Davis 15, 45
UC Davis School of Medicine 15
UC Riverside 45
UNC - Chapel Hill 45
UNC Eshelman School of Pharmacy 90
UNCF 13, 15, 114, 117, 118, 119
United Negro College Fund xvi, 13, 15, 117
University of Alabama at Birmingham
    Heersink School of Medicine 52
University of Arkansas at Pine Bluff 65, 118
University of Buffalo SUNY Jacobs School of
    Medicine 52
University of California's 2024 Statement on
    Mathematics 4
University of Chicago 45
University of Colorado Hospital ix
University of Connecticut Medical School
    45, 49
University of Florida College of Medicine 51
University of Florida College of Nursing 66
University of Glasgow xx
University of Kentucky 49
University of Kentucky College of Medicine
    49
University of Maryland - Baltimore County 9
University of Maryland Eastern Shore 44, 99,
    109, 112
University of Maryland Eastern Shore
    Physician Assistant Department 44
University of Maryland Eastern Shore School
    of Pharmacy and Health Professions 88
University of Maryland Eastern Shore School
    of Veterinary Medicine 109
University of Maryland School of Dentistry
    35
University of Mississippi Medical Center 67
University of Mississippi Pharmacy School 90
University of Missouri-St. Louis College of
    Optometry 75
University of North Carolina - Chapel Hill
    Adams School of Dentistry 35
University of Pennsylvania 21, 34
University of Rochester 51, 67
University of South Alabama College of
    Medicine 52
University of Southern California Dental

School 36
University of the Virgin Islands 47, 122
University of Virginia x
University of Wisconsin Rural and Urban
    Scholars in Community Health 19, 51
University of Wisconsin School of Medicine
    and Public Health 19
Upstate Accelerated Scholars 47
Urban Medicine and Public Health 19
U.S. Bureau of Labor Statistics Occupational
    Outlook Handbook vii, 23, 29, 40, 75
USC 13, 102, 103
U.S. Department of Education xvi, xix
U.S. News and World Reports 11
U.S. News & World Reports 45
UVA Health 9
UW–Madison 19
UW-Milwaukee 19
UW-Parkside 19
UW-Platteville 19

**V**

Vanderbilt 21, 45, 51
Vanderbilt School of Medicine 45, 51
Veronica Anderson 4
Virginia Commonwealth University School of
    Medicine 48
Virginia State University 7, 90
Virginia Tech Carilion School of Medicine 48
Virginia Union University 47
VSP Vision 78

**W**

Washington University in St. Louis 21
Wayna Wondwossen 6
Wesleyan University 4
What HBCUs Can Teach Us About Culturally
    Sustaining Practices 1
Which undergrad majors are best for med
    school? 14
White House 22
Why the U.S. Needs More Black Physicians ix
Why we need more Black doctors ix
Winston-Salem State 63, 64, 65, 66, 99
Wisconsin Academy for Rural Medicine 19
Wright State University 45

**X**

Xavier-Mayo Alliance 53
Xavier University of Louisiana xiv, xviii, 4, 9,
    13, 15, 20, 21, 36, 41, 44, 46, 49, 53, 54,
    67, 75, 89, 90, 102
Xavier University of Louisiana College of
    Pharmacy 89

**Y**

Yale Summer Undergraduate Research

                    Mychal Wynn

Fellowship Program  19

**Z**

Zippia  105
Zucker School of Medicine  52
Zucker School of Medicine Pipeline Program
    52

For current pricing and to order copies of the books in this series:

*Order on-line at www.rspublishing.com*
*Order by phone at 770.518.0369*

To purchase large quantities, request quantity discounts, or to order a special printing for your state, school district, or high school:

*Email: info@rspublishing.com*
*Phone: 770.518.0369*
*Rising Sun Publishing*
*P.O. Box 70906*
*Marietta, GA 30007-0906*

Books in the *Why Attend an HBCU* series:

**Vol: I Why Attend an HBCU**
*ISBN 13: 978-1-880463-54-3 | 5.5 x 8.5 | 128 pages*
*Available on Amazon Kindle*

**Vol: II HBCU Healthcare Pathways**
*ISBN 13: 978-1-880463-55-0 | 5.5 x 8.5 | 160 pages*
*Available on Amazon Kindle*

**Vol: III HBCU STEM Pathways**
*ISBN 13: 978-1-880463-57-4 | 5.5 x 8.5 | 128 pages*
*Available on Amazon Kindle*

**HBCU Scholarships and more...***
*ISBN 13: 978-1-880463-24-3 | 8.5 x 11 | 384 pages*

www.ingramcontent.com/pod-product-compliance
Lightning Source LLC
Chambersburg PA
CBHW060929050726
47592CB00003B/876